FINDING
THE
STILL POINT

TOM HARPUR

FINDING THE STILL POINT

A Spiritual Response to Stress

Northstone

Editor: Michael Schwartzentruber
Cover and interior design: Margaret Kyle
Cover photo: Copyright © 2000 Jan Phillips from her book *God Is at Eye Level: Photography as a Healing Art*, www.janphillips.com. Used with permission.

Unless otherwise noted, all biblical quotations are from the New Revised Standard Version of the Bible, copyright © 1989 by the Division of Christian Education of the National Council of Churches of Christ in the United States of America, and are used by permission. All rights reserved.

The letters KJV signify the King James Version.

Northstone Publishing acknowledges the financial support of the Government of Canada through the Book Publishing Industry Development Program for its publishing activities.

Northstone Publishing is an imprint of Wood Lake Books Inc., an employee-owned company, and is committed to caring for the environment and all creation. Northstone recycles and reuses and encourages readers to do the same. Resources are printed on recycled paper and more environmentally friendly groundwood papers (newsprint), whenever possible. The trees used are replaced through donations to the Scoutrees For Canada Program. A portion of all profit is donated to charitable organizations.

National Library of Canada Cataloguing in Publication Data
Harpur, Tom
Finding the still point: the spirituality of balance/Tom Harpur.
Originally published, 2002, with subtitle: A spiritual response to stress.
Includes bibliographical references and index.
ISBN 1-896836-71-2
1. Stress (Psychology) – Religious aspects – Christianity.
2. Meditation – Christianity.   3. Spiritual life – Christianity.   I. Title
BV4501.3H37   2004a   248.4   C2004-906065-1

Published by Northstone Publishing,
an imprint of Wood Lake Books Publishing Inc.
Kelowna, British Columbia, Canada

Printing 10 9 8 7 6 5 4 3 2 1
Printed in Canada at Transcontinental

DEDICATION
For my sisters
Elizabeth and Jane

At the still point of the turning world.
Neither flesh nor fleshless;
Neither from nor towards;
At the still point, there the dance is,....

T. S. Eliot, *Four Quartets – Burnt Norton*

CONTENTS

INTRODUCTION

Thank God our time is now, when wrong
Comes up to face us everywhere,
Never to leave us 'til we take
The longest stride of soul man ever took.
Affairs are now soul size.
The enterprise is exploration into God.

Christopher Fry

Nobody who was over the age of five or six on the morning of September 11, 2001, will ever forget the shock, fear, grief, anger, and utter confusion engendered on that day. The anti-American terrorists' sudden, merciless, and self-annihilating attacks on the huge towers of the World Trade Center in New York, and on the Pentagon in Washington, set off such a wholly unprecedented series of aftershocks and repercussions that the world has not been, and likely never will be completely, the same again. Virtually everything we have ever known has been affected in some way. This includes our way of thinking about the nature of God; the relationship of every religion, but particularly of Christianity, Judaism, and Islam, to each other and to all other religions;

and the role of faith and spirituality themselves in the world in the days and years ahead.

The purpose of this volume is not an analysis of those world-shaking events. But they, of necessity, will color and provide the context of much that it contains. A lot of the research and some of the writing of this book on stress had already been begun just before the September 11 cataclysm. I am writing this introduction, indeed, less than a couple of months following the tragedy and President George W. Bush's declaration of America's and her coalition of allies' "War Against Terrorism." Fresh alarms, warnings of possible future terrorist attacks, and discoveries of deliberately modified anthrax germs keep being trumpeted through the media as I write.

The truth is that one of the biggest consequences of all that has happened, and still is happening, has been an exponential increase in an already chronic problem in Western culture and society. Tension, anxiety, fear, and panic, and their manifold, complex, mental, emotional, and physical effects on human health and happiness are ancient human problems. But in the so-called post-modern era, since about the end of World War II, their presence and potency for misery have grown so markedly that they constituted a huge health and well-being crisis even before the September 11 terrorists overturned the world. Thus, there surely has never been a more urgent need for fresh thinking about stress than there is today.

This book focuses on a spiritual approach to stress. That's what makes it most different from almost all of the current flood of self-help manuals. There are, as we shall see, many effective methods and techniques being developed to combat the more devastating and debilitating symptoms of stress, as well as the lesser consequences which manifest themselves, nevertheless, in a loss of productivity, creativity, and general wellness in the lives of millions of ordinary folk. As an aside, it is the belief of a number of experts in the field that the ability of our human nervous system to adapt –

our basic body/emotion/mind/spirit constitution, developed and tested over innumerable millennia – may have well reached its outer limits for the increasing speed, change, and complexity of modern living. In other words, evolution itself in the hands of God has not fully prepared us for what our technology has catapulted us into. We know much more about the external world than we do of our own internal world and there are many signs around us of people cracking with total breakdown or burnout. There was a clear example of what I'm talking about in *The Toronto Star* front section, on October 23, 2001. The headline read, "'Canadian workers stressed,' study says." The Canadian Press story described how world uncertainty following the September 11, 2001, terrorist attacks may be "the final straw" for a workforce already beaten down by years of downsizing, job uncertainty, longer working hours, and the sheer glut of information to be handled. The study, by two university professors, one at Carleton University, Ottawa, and the other from the University of Western Ontario, in London, Ontario, said: "Your workload is increasing, your stress is already high and you don't know if there is going to be a tomorrow. Work satisfaction in Canada has dropped to 45 percent in 2001 from 62 percent in 1991. Also, in 2001 only 50 percent were 'highly committed' to their jobs compared to 66 percent a decade ago." This report follows a recent Ipsos-Reid poll, done for *The Globe and Mail* and CTV, which found that one in three Canadians is anxious or irritable due to the uncertain future caused by the war on terrorism and threats of more terrorist attacks to come. A quarter of the population, one in four Canadians, reported they are "always" or "often" stressed and overwhelmed since September 11, 2001, and the attacks. Similar polls in the U.S. reveal that the impact of these events is even more profound there.

Yet now, at the same time, ancient wisdoms, together with exciting new scientific findings, are combining to show why it is that mere coping techniques in general – and especially for meeting the stress crisis – are not enough. Divorced from their spiritual underpinnings and/or religious understanding, such techniques, applied to stress, lack a potency which they were originally designed to have and meant to impart.

This is the main argument here: spirituality, plus the practice of mind/body methods or techniques, is a far more powerful antidote to the phenomena accompanying all that is summed up in the term "stress" than either medicines (though they have a richly deserved place) or regular stress-coping disciplines by themselves. It is the spirituality aspect that makes all the difference.

This leads me immediately to the other argument or thesis put forward in what follows. It has to do with continuing themes in all my thinking and writing: what is true spirituality, what is the role and the relevancy of religion in our world, and, in particular, is there any future for the Christian church?

There can be no doubt, since September 11, 2001, that all religions must change, that they must begin to see and emphasize the huge assets, moral and spiritual, which they have in common. They must become a major part of the answer to global tensions instead of too frequently being a cause or at least a serious part of them. Rather than concentrating, as in the past, on visions of another world beyond, or even on the imperialistic aim of eventually lording it over all other faiths in this one, their relevance must be demonstrated through a more practical approach to humanity's deepest needs. This moment in history, I believe, is their unique opportunity.

But what about the faith that has been predominantly that of the Western world – at least nominally so, though it is common nowadays to talk of the "post-Christian era"? While Christianity may well be thriving in parts of Africa and Latin America, statistics on declining membership in Europe, Canada, and even the more showily religious United States of America, reveal an alarming trend. The former Bishop of Newark, New Jersey, the Rt. Rev. John Spong, contends that "the church must change or die." What's more, it's difficult, if not impossible, to challenge this assertion. Most of his arguments about everything from our outdated concepts of God – all ideas and propositions about God become outdated as soon as they have become too-precisely formulated – to the Virgin Birth, the Atonement, and, beyond that, back to the myths about Original Sin and the "Fall" of Adam and Eve, are cogent and call for a well-considered response from his fellow bishops immediately.

But while church leaders and others ponder this crisis for orthodoxy and for the traditional creeds, and while they make plans to meet it, ordinary people both outside and within Western organized religion still need to be ministered to. They are searching for some solid food and drink for the soul while they are still being offered – too often – either ecclesiastical nonsense or popular pap. While Spong and others who think and feel as he does are busily breaking the eggs for an as-yet-unknown religious "omelette," many people are left asking what, if anything, is left of any "Good News" or gospel to be experienced and to be made known?

I am certain myself that – though important changes do indeed need to be made regarding the creeds especially – there is a very great deal remaining to be shared. But the official churches of the right, left, and full center are for the most part bent on ignoring their full spiritual inheritance. One of the supreme ironies of all time is the way in which most of the growing-edge, vital trends and themes of life today (for example, holistic healing; the bond between spirituality and health; the relationship of body energy fields and traditional medicine; meditation; stress-reduction books, tapes, and seminars; as well as pilgrimages sacred or secular, and a deep love and caring for the Earth itself) are already a part of the Christian heritage and tradition. They have, in fact, been so for nearly 2,000 years.

Here and there they are being rediscovered within the church, but, for the most part, they lie like forgotten treasures in an attic. When they pop up in occasional Bible readings during worship, or get featured treatment in the mass media, they are passed over in silence or treated as though they were somehow "New Age" and thus to be scorned or condemned. As my mother was wont to say about things she disliked, "It's as if they came from the devil himself."

The tragedy of this profound misunderstanding (yes, and stupidity too) on the part of the church is that secular systems have been able to cash in on this neglect and to usurp assets that properly belong to Christianity and to most other faiths as well. But as the famous preacher St. John Chrysostom (c. 347–407 CE and the Bishop of Constantinople at his death) once said many hundreds of years ago, the church is like a woman who had once a magnificent jewel case in which she kept her most precious gems. The gems – healing, "miracles," meditation, hope, wholeness, true renewal and inner peace – are now all gone. Only the empty jewel case, the relatively unimportant shell, remains, he lamented.

This book is an attempt to search for and examine one of these great lost jewels – the spiritual path for coping and dealing with stress, worry, and anxiety. Stress, I repeat, is the leading problem of our time. To think, talk, and act meaningfully and helpfully about it is to touch a common chord in all of us. It is to "bite" into an issue that in turn "bites" everyone, including all the would-be healers themselves. For that reason, stress could and should be a major concern of church strategy. It should be a leading topic for sermons, seminars, retreats, study groups, and religious TV.

Stress will always be with us. *Finding the Still Point* and its suggestions are offered in the conviction, gained from personal experience that, with regard to stress, the spiritual path is ultimately the only one that really works in depth. The church (or temple, or synagogue, or other holy shrine) that proclaims this kind of message will never suffer from empty pews. It may well still need to change, but it will not die.

My deepest hope, though, is that for you, as it has for myself, this book will prove to be an "exploration into God." That is our greatest need.

PART ONE

THE
CONTEMPORARY
SCENE

I

THE CHRONIC STRESS
OF MODERN LIVING

If you are currently not experiencing any stress in your life,
you should immediately lie down –
it appears you may be dead.
Allen Klein, *The Courage to Laugh*[1]

Life is stressful. Consequently, stress is inevitable for us all. It's the stuff of living itself. Without it, the entire evolutionary development of the "higher" animals, and of humans in particular, would never have taken place in the way it has done. The biological "fight or flight" syndrome, over millions of years, has been a powerful factor not just in our overall survival, but in our gradual discovering and mastering of all the special skills which make our species unique. One can even go so far as to affirm that stress – physical, emotional, mental, and spiritual – has been a remarkable "tool" in the whole creation process.

Consider, for example, the most constant and unvarying truth about our universe. It is, of course, as Heraclitus said long ago, the fact of change: "Everything flows or is in flux," he affirmed. We know that nothing has or ever will happen, whether small or large in the scale of things, without change. But change is a recognized, major cause of stress at every stage of human life. We fear change as a species and this very fear is itself a symptom of stress.

However, to speak of the "symptoms of stress" or of stress as a problem is already to have given away the reality that while it has been and can be a positive agent for progress and development – for example, the jack rabbit's long legs and incredible running stamina developed as it was pursued by a variety of shrewd and speedy predators – stress has been, on the whole, viewed by our species as a negative, painful and even destructive aspect of human experience. There are a myriad of valid reasons why this is the case. The great Rishis or holy men of the Himalayas, for thousands of years BCE; the founders of the major religions; the Stoics and the Epicureans of ancient Greece and, later, of the Roman Empire; philosophers, spiritual thinkers, theologians and saints, scientists, and millions of others from the earliest days – all have realized that happiness, peace of mind, calmness, freedom from the fret of worry and anxiety, are not just the marks of a fully human life. They are directly threatened and often ruined by excessive stress. In an existence in which randomness and chance can never be ruled out or controlled, no matter how successful our attempts to master our environment may be, the choice is not one of stress or no stress at all. It's a matter of *how* each one of us responds to the stresses life presents to us. In *The Globe and Mail* poll cited in the introduction, the researchers found that while a small percentage of Canadians (16 percent) felt they were coping well with the changed situation since the September 11 attacks and their aftermath, another small group were discovered to have been "completely unhinged" by the same events. This is obviously not a simple matter for interpretation, but it does show that *how* things are viewed and dealt with makes an enormous difference.

This, of course, does not mean that we have utterly no control over some of the stressors in our lives. For example, we often deliberately take on more than any average human being can handle. (Too many speaking engagements on top of other responsibilities have been a temptation for me.) Whether through vanity, competitiveness, love of fame, money, or a better self-image, or whether from an insufficient commitment to our own health and well-being, we often become our own worst enemies, sabotaging our best intentions by not examining our behaviors and motives closely enough. Only *you* can end the stresses you deliberately bring upon yourself. It doesn't take much insight to realize that if you watch CNN for hours before going to bed, it's unlikely you'll have an early or satisfying sleep.

That had to be said. But it does nothing to change the fundamental situation being described. Too much stress, whether self-inflicted or necessity-inflicted, can be a painful, dangerous thing. The huge difference between ourselves and those who concerned themselves with the causes of human suffering over the past millennia is that medical science can now document the destructive impact of high or chronic stress on our entire organism – and thus its total negative consequences for our society and overall future as well.

We don't need a catalogue of statistics here. Through the media, and no doubt through the tough school of personal experience, nearly everybody today knows what at least some of the principal symptoms and results of stress, not handled well, can be.

These include insomnia, inability to concentrate, debilitation of the immune system, chronic anxiety, panic attacks, depression, loss of appetite and weight, over-eating and obesity, diarrhoea, constipation, and ulcers – a virtually endless litany of ills. The losses of human productivity resulting from all of these can be calculated and are enormous. In a column in *The Globe and Mail*, on October 11, 2001, Madeleine Drohan documented some of the costs. In the article, titled "Technology Comes with a Price: Stress and Depression," she told how the Canadian Business and Economic Roundtable on Mental Health and the International Labour Organization had presented a report in

Geneva that same week on the scope of the problem and its impact in terms of dollars. The report estimated that businesses in Europe and North America lose $120 billion (U.S.) each year because of stress, depression, and other mental health disorders among employees. That figure includes lost productivity, increased disability insurance claims, and lower performance and innovation. Yet the forfeiture of human happiness or contentment involved really cannot be measured. The number of heart attacks in the Western world caused by stress is calculable; the same is true of other conditions named above. But nobody can begin to measure the huge increase worldwide in the stress and misery caused by the grief, anxiety, panic, destruction, maimings, homelessness, and hunger wrought by the unprecedented lessons in terror we are presently heirs to.

There is so much more. Studies done in the United States and Canada reveal that North Americans in particular began showing increased signs of stress and a need for professional help for all sorts of anxiety-related symptoms immediately after the terrorist attacks on New York and the Pentagon. In Canada, to meet this need, a country-wide medical network was set up within days of the tragedy. It included Health Canada, the Canadian Medical Association (CMA), and ten other professional groups. The network has been trying to make Canadians more aware of the difference between normal reactions to tragedies, losses and other stresses, and the point where full professional assistance is needed. (The Internet address is www.cma.ca/cmhsn)

Nobody, even those so thick-skinned or so involved in themselves that they feel little for others in any case, is wholly immune to the adverse effects of stress in our daily lives. Some have better coping skills than others, but every one of us is vulnerable at some point – or even at many points. Our daily newspapers, magazines, and TV specials are regularly filled with specific cases – concerning especially the rich (not necessarily in money) and the famous. As an admitted ice hockey fan, I usually glance at the sports pages of the morning paper. Today, there was an article that referred to a *Sports Illustrated* feature[2] in which one of the toughest forwards for The Toronto Maple Leafs, Shayne Corson, spoke out publicly for the first time about severe panic attacks he suffered during the 2000–2001 NHL season. "I'd feel like I was having a heart attack," Corson told the magazine. "It was like everything was coming down on me at once. I didn't want to be away from home; I didn't want to be in crowds. It fed on itself, you know? The more scared I got, the more guilty I felt about being scared. I wanted to be strong." Corson, knowing he risked ridicule from the many thousands of would-be macho "jocks" who make up a large proportion of the hockey-watching community, added that there were nights that season when he couldn't hold back the tears. He said, "Much too often I'd wake up in the middle of the night panicking. My heart would be pounding, tears in my eyes. I wouldn't know what to do." He credited his roommate (on the road trips) who also happens to be his brother-in-law, Darcy Tucker, for helping him get through the attacks and for helping him get well. "I don't think I'd have made it if Tucker hadn't been my roommate," he said. Tucker reportedly told the magazine that there were "a couple of nights" when he thought seriously of taking Corson to the hospital. Corson, who says he has no idea of what brought on the attacks in the first place, described his recovery as a "long and gradual process" during which he regularly consulted a psychiatrist and took prescribed medication. He said things were "much better" this season, but added, "Panic is something I'll always have to deal with."

Corson's problem is far from unique. It's growing and almost endemic in the Western world, where for so long the chief emphasis has been on "doing" rather than on "being." He is certainly to be highly commended for having the courage to admit his weakness in this respect. His honesty may well help many others, men in particular, to deal with the stress and panic in their lives too.

There is no doubt that life is moving too speedily for us, that changes are coming far faster than our parents and their parents before them could ever have dreamed in moments of fantasy, and that this is a major source of stress. Some scientists are even putting forward a thesis which I don't accept yet, but which is becoming harder to refute. Specifically, they say that the rate of change and hence the level of stress is testing or even surpassing our evolutionary limits. Having become human "doers" instead of human "beings" through an enslavement to external forces – largely technology, convenience, and speed – we are arriving quickly, or indeed may have already arrived, at a place where the human organism was never designed to go.

A news story datelined Atlanta, by Cox Newspapers, July 27, 2001, tends to confirm this conclusion. The article documents the way in which the "Information Age," with its all-pervasive technology and speed, is overwhelming us with its concomitant stress. It quoted a Reuters News Agency survey of 1998 in which one-third of the respondents (made up of 1,300 business professionals in the United States, Britain, and Asia) said they suffered from stress-related health problems brought on by too much information. Forty-three percent said they had difficulty making important decisions and nearly two-thirds said even their personal relationships suffered because of the overload. Mental health experts, according to Reuters, have now come up with a fresh disorder – "information fatigue syndrome." Its symptoms are very familiar: depression, anxiety, insomnia, inability to focus, headaches, high blood pressure, and social withdrawal. There is little or no time for care of one's soul, for wise thoughts, for self-nurture.

In his book *The Social Life of Information*,[3] John Seely Brown says that on an average weekday alone, a major newspaper contains more information than any contemporary of Shakespeare's would have acquired in a lifetime. "There's no way human sensory evolution has caught up with that kind of deluge," he says.

True, e-mail, cellphones, fax machines, "digital this and that" all make for an exciting, swiftly connected lifestyle, but for those interested in pursuing the darker side of this I recommend James Gleick's book *Faster: The Acceleration of Just About Everything*.[4]

In a comment included in the *Globe* feature by Madeleine Drohan, mentioned earlier, Gleick says, "Everything comes with costs. More information and more connectedness mean more stress. You still have to decide what your priorities are. You still have to choose, and choosing amid greater chaos is very difficult."

LIVING TO BE 100 YEARS OLD

To reinforce the same point another way, it's worthwhile pausing for a few moments to examine some findings reported in the November 2001 issue of the monthly *Johns Hopkins Medical Letter*. It contains a cover story called "Health after 100: Secrets of the Centenarians." It notes that centenarians are among the fastest growing – and healthiest – of age groups in the United States. "Today, 75,000 Americans are aged 100 or over," the feature says. "If current trends continue, their numbers will double every 10 years. Contrary to popular belief, they are often in better shape than their younger counterparts: 30 percent show so few signs of disability that they continue living independently and 40 percent more are able to function well despite some limitations. The remaining 30 percent…require daily care."

Certainly genes are important, the article reports. "However, many experts think that genetic influences are strongest after age 80. Before that, they say, lifestyle factors are more significant." The evidence for this view comes largely from studies of older twins, "which indicate that lifestyle accounts for about two-thirds of age-related disabilities that shorten life, with genes accounting for the remaining third." Thomas Perls, M.D., M.P.H., lead investigator of the ongoing New England Centenarian Study (it's following 1,000 centenarians), says that people who take the

right steps can add as many as ten quality years to their lives –
and those who don't bother can subtract a decade.

Longevity studies in not just the U.S. and Sweden but in
several other countries as well now show what these measures
should be. Take, for example, the Okinawan Centenarian Study
(OCS), which focused on 600 centenarians and many people in
their 70s, 80s, and 90s from Okinawa, and which was printed in
the *Johns Hopkins Medical Letter* mentioned above. This Japanese
archipelago, in the Pacific between the islands of Japan and Tai-
wan, has the highest per capita concentration of centenarians and
the longest disability-free lifespan in the world: "Okinawans have
80 percent fewer heart attacks than Americans," the article in the
medical letter says. "And because *prostate and breast cancers are so rare*,
screening for these malignancies is not routine" (italics mine).

These are astounding statistics. Where do Okinawan lifestyles
differ from those of North American and the rest of the so-
called developed world?

1. *Diet*. This is an obvious factor. Okinawans eat very little harm-
   ful saturated fat, or other fats in general. The average Okinawan
   eats daily about seven servings of vegetables and fruits; seven
   servings of whole grains, mostly brown rice and noodles; and
   at least two servings of soy (beans or *miso*). Fish or tiny amounts
   of meat may also be included. This plant-based diet provides
   lots of fiber, thus lowering heart disease, strokes, diabetes, and
   digestive-tract cancers. They eat plenty of soy, which is rich
   in calcium and isoflavones, a type of carotene which can help
   increase bone density, lower cholesterol, and "possibly reduce
   the risk of some cancers."
2. *Exercise*. Where North Americans over-depend on their cars
   and spend an amazing amount of time sitting down,
   Okinawans have vigorous physical activity, mainly walking
   or biking, as an integral part of daily life and they live this
   way throughout their later years. The benefits of regular ac-

tivity are well-known – lowering of cholesterol; prevention of obesity, diabetes, heart disease, stroke, and osteoarthritis; and so much more.

3. *Smoking.* Few Okinawans smoke. Those who drink alcoholic beverages do so moderately, averaging 1 or 2 drinks a day. (We live in small-town Canada and are constantly amazed at the high prevalence of smoking in spite of all the warnings against it. Young and old alike seem addicted.)

4. *Stress, attitude, and outlook.* Centenarian studies everywhere show the great importance for longevity of how people respond to stress. Scientists have proven that there is a direct connection between stress levels and heart disease and depression, for example. How people cope with stress – from a minor incident such as a traffic snarl to a major event such as the loss of a loved one – can impact negatively on human health. The elderly Okinawans of the quoted study are optimistic in outlook, tend to be self-confident, and score low in time-urgency and tension categories. Communal support is an essential feature of Okinawan society. A major proverb there states that "one cannot live in this world without the support of others." The study shows that elders who avail themselves of the "connecting circle" and other common-purpose meetings, which are a part of their culture, live longer than those without ties to family, friends, or colleagues.

5. *Spirituality.* By far the most significant finding is the healing role of spirituality. The report says that spirituality is "a key aspect of Okinawan life – particularly among the elders: It underlies everyday activities (even gardening is viewed as a religious experience as plants are thought to be imbued with spirit) and all health practices." Okinawans see their doctor for physical problems and their shamans for any 'spiritual imbalances' that might be contributing to them. Prayer is of signal importance. They pray for longevity, among other blessings. The *Johns Hopkins Medical Letter* then adds: "Western

studies have shown that prayer triggers the relaxation response, lowers blood pressure and heart rate *and is a powerful stress reducer.*" Dozens of recent research projects have confirmed and expanded on these positive results.[5]

All of this has been confirmed independently in studies done at the University of Toronto. Researchers there, reviewing population health surveys, contend that up to 43,000 deaths a year in Canada are due to low levels of spirituality. They define spirituality as the beliefs we hold concerning our place in the universe and our connection to a higher power. Spirituality, they found, reduces stress, promotes healthy lifestyle choices, and increases a sense of belonging – all links to lower mortality.[6]

By looking at the factors leading to longevity and to better quality of life in the latter years of life, we have caught our first glimpse of how various steps – particularly in the spiritual realm – deliberately acknowledged and taken can and do make all the difference where stress is concerned. The modern medical response, however, is important and must be examined next.

II

THE MEDICAL RESPONSE

Prayer indeed is good,
but while calling on the gods
a man should himself lend a hand.
Hippocrates, the "Father of Medicine," c. 460–400 BCE

Since stress and stress-related ills are a major and fast-growing source of pain, suffering, and – in worst-case scenarios such as depression, "burnout," heart attacks and stroke – of cessation of any ability to function, obviously doctors and medical scientists are devoting more and more time to the best way of dealing with this threat to well-being. Extraordinary progress has been made and the future seems bright with promise. Dr. John Evans, a former Rhodes Scholar and leading research specialist, said in a speech to the Canadian Psychiatric Research Foundation in December 2001: "There has been an explosion of knowledge on how to fight mental illness using technology such as imaging machines and devices that allow exquisitely sensitive detection of protein in the brain." He underlined the fact that research has shown that often mental illness is caused by something genetic or biological and is not within a person's power to control on their own.

Since I am not a scientist or a doctor, and because the chief concern of this book is about a spiritual response to stress as an additional, much more holistic approach than that of traditional medicine, I don't intend to repeat here what can be discovered and known through a multitude of other means. Bookstores, the media, and the medical journals are literally inundated with stories of the latest medications for anxiety, panic attacks, and the various kinds of depressive illnesses. Physical fitness routines, special diets, as well as gimmicks of all kinds and self-help books galore, have become whole new industries for a consumer culture that is most susceptible to the prospect of instant remedies for all stress-making complexities. Sales of "natural remedies" – many of proven worth and yet many more with few or no credentials whatever, the so-called "evidence" being 100 percent anecdotal – have skyrocketed all about us.

There can be no doubt that the present medical approach has relieved a vast amount of suffering and pain. There is a solid place for anti-stress and anti-depression medications and the cornucopia of other new pharmaceutical remedies in the medical establishment's present arsenal. But there are some great difficulties with this overall strategy and its practice as well.

The one striking thing that most people say when you ask them about their level of satisfaction with their family doctor or other medical persons at clinics, laboratories, or hospitals, is that "everybody is in too much of a rush." Asked to draw a picture of his doctor, a 5-year-old boy who had been in hospital for several weeks told the therapist, "That's easy!" He took pencil and paper and worked for less than two minutes, What he produced was a series of shaded blurs! The average time spent by patients in a doctor's office in Canada today is about eight minutes or less. Since the doctor's income comes from the national health plan, on a per capita basis – a sort of assembly-line piecework –

there is little incentive to slow down. By the time the doctor greets the patient, asks what the problem is, does a swift examination, and writes out the expected prescription (patients still tend to think that a consultation that doesn't end with a prescription has been a waste of everybody's time), there is very little opportunity for an adequate discussion of the specific symptoms, and none at all for an exploration of what's really going on in the patient's life.

Dr. Carl Gustav Jung (1875–1961), the famous psychoanalyst, once observed that in about 80 percent of his patients the true, underlying cause of their trouble stemmed from a "spiritual problem" and not a purely mental or emotional one at all. Unfortunately, even though there are some small signs of possible change (almost a third of medical schools in North America now have a course on spirituality), the traditional medical model leaves out the spiritual dimension almost entirely.

Despite all that is known now about how our bodies, minds, and emotions all interact intimately with one another; despite the enormous insights gained in psychiatry, psychology, and various "cognitive therapies" developed since Freud; despite the success, since it was first recognized and given a name in 1977, of the new, more holistic Behavioral Science approach (a mind/body paradigm), medicine in Western countries is still largely wedded to a view of the body as a kind of machine. We call this the mechanistic view. The patient is, in a sense, irrelevant to the process of tinkering with the machine. The analogy of a mechanic with a car is fairly accurate. Fresh oil, better gas, new tires, even a new engine – the list of possibilities is only limited to what a modern hospital can supply to ailing persons through replacements surgeries, transplants, and the like. Most of the growing dissatisfaction with healthcare today, however, is that it too often still leaves the patient feeling like an object, a "piece of meat," in short, as a machine. Stress that is relieved by pills without any further reference to its causes or to tools for coping with it is poorly handled indeed. It deals only with symptoms while ignoring the root causes. Instead of enabling the patient to grow and to use the experience to learn more about life and him or herself, the process keeps the patient infantilized and dependent.

BEHAVIORAL MEDICINE

It was suggested above that a change or shift of paradigm is nevertheless under way and gradually seeping down from the experts and researchers to the doctors on the front lines. The idea that you cannot treat the body without treating the mind and vice versa is truly a very ancient one. As the Bible says, in Proverbs 17:21:

A cheerful heart is a good medicine,
but a downcast spirit dries up the bones.

The old Latin tag, *Mens sana in corpore sano* (a healthy mind in a healthy body), asserts a similar point. What makes the present "breakthrough" so significant is that our vastly increased knowledge of the most subtle workings of both mind and body gives a reliable scientific basis for what previously was based wholly upon observation and intuition. We knew the truth of the biblical proverb, "As a person thinks, so is he," but we didn't know accurately just how this works. "Perhaps the most fundamental development in Behavioral Medicine is the recognition that we can no longer think about health as being solely a characteristic of the body or the mind because body and mind are interconnected," says Jon Kabat-Zinn, Ph.D., Director of the Stress Reduction Clinic at the University of Massachusetts Medical Center. Kabat-Zinn, who is the author of two best-selling books on his behavioralist approach, which focuses largely on the application of the principles of meditation and Hatha yoga, goes on to say that, "The new perspective acknowledges the central importance of thinking in terms of wholeness and interconnectedness and the need to pay attention to the interactions of mind, body, and behavior in efforts to understand and treat illness." He gives eloquent testimony to the way in which medicine today is presently expanding its own working model of what health and illness are and "how lifestyle, patterns of thinking and feeling, relationships, and environmental factors all interact to influence health."[1]

We'll examine Kabat-Zinn's full, stress clinic approach to our central concern in a moment, but it's important to make a brief criticism at this point. I heard Kabat-Zinn give several lectures in San Francisco in the spring of 1997 and have greatly enjoyed both of his books, *Full Catastrophe Living* and *Wherever You Go, There You Are*. They should be required reading for all therapists and doctors. But, in my view, they don't go far enough. While pleading for a holistic approach to health, he and the majority of behavioralists like him still manage to perpetuate a truncated paradigm of human beings and of how the whole organism of human-"beingness" works. The body-mind model is certainly better than that of the body on its own, treated as an object – something that has been with us since the philosopher René Descartes. But it cannot be emphasized too much that it is still shorn of a powerful aspect – the spiritual dimension. A human being is not simply a body and mind interacting and deeply interconnected. We are above all spiritual animals and can never find full wholeness until the paradigm becomes one of body, mind, and spirit. That is the thesis of this book, which will be developed in detail shortly.

But to show my real feelings and beliefs on when and how I think modern medicine should be applied even to the most spiritual of people – in case anyone has inferred so far that there is some bias here against traditional medicine and/or drugs – I want to conclude this chapter with a condensation of a column I wrote for *The Toronto Sunday Star* (October 28, 2001).

Many people were surprised to see the headline in

The Toronto Star about the "saint" of Calcutta. It read: "Darkness Haunted Mother Teresa." It told how this outwardly calm, steadfast, almost stoical embodiment of Christian humility and sacrificial service – a Nobel Prize winner in 1979 and, presently a "contender" for beatification, the first official step on the road to official sainthood – was harassed all her adult life with depression and a feeling of God's absence.

In an intimate, self-portrait-in-words, her spiritual diaries and letters, just published by an Indian theological journal, the *Vidyajyoti* (Light of Knowledge), the epitome of Christian discipleship reveals starkly how for most of her life in Calcutta she felt abandoned by God, unworthy of God's love, and sometimes even doubted God's existence. She confesses that often the darkness was so great she could not pray.

She was frequently tempted to quit the ministry she had begun in 1946 by founding a religious order – the Missionaries of Charity – to care for the poor and the dying not just in India but eventually in many other desperate places around the world.

She wrote: "I feel darkness, that surrounds me on all sides. I can't lift up my soul to God: No light, no inspiration enters my soul."

In the end, like Paul and other mystics through the centuries, she won a kind of victory over her affliction. She had come, by the 1990s, to begin "to love my darkness, for I believe now it is a part, a very small part, of Jesus' darkness and pain on Earth." Her suffering, she explained, brought her closer to her Lord even though it seldom *lifted*.

A friend of hers, Rev. Joseph Neuner who wrote the feature article, while noting that some experience of darkness and depression has been part of virtually every spiritual life, commented that "it may be difficult to find a parallel to the lifelong night which enwrapped Mother Teresa." Certainly the "dark night of the soul" is a common enough experience for those truly seeking to know and serve God. But its depth and length in this case is surely pathological. What a great pity that her doctors failed to diagnose her obvious depression and that modern antidepressants had not yet been discovered/engineered. She should, however, have been treated by a psychiatrist and given whatever relief was available.

Out of suffering, sometimes blessings can come. But there's little value in unnecessary suffering per se, in spite of what some of the pious say. Had she been properly cared for and had she improved as a result it would no more detract from her saintliness than taking a beta-blocker or other medicine for her weak heart.

Many Canadians suffer from aging, illness, and difficulty sleeping, as Mother Teresa did. It's a part of the human condition to be relieved with compassion, prayer, and the best in medical care.

The new cognitive therapies, quite often attended by various prescribed medications, at least in the initial stages of treatment, are, in my reading and study, one of the best tools the medical community has at its disposal today. By "cognitive" is meant the use of a rational approach to the patient's problems. The stressed-out patient is helped and encouraged to think about the patterns of behavior and thought that he or she uses in coping with daily life. Unhelpful or destructive habits of mind are laid bare and practical alternatives offered. Coupled with what I describe in the rest of the book, cognitive therapy can be powerful enough to change lives in a radical way.

III

THE MEDITATION
RESPONSE

Breathing is the key to living a spiritual life in physical embodiment.
When the body dies, the breath leaves the body.
Where does it go?
Most of you think the body is the creator of the breath.
Actually, it is the other way around.
The breath is the begetter of the body.
When the breath goes, the body ceases to function.
It disintegrates into nothing because,
without the breath of spirit, the body is nothing.

Paul Ferrini, *Silence of the Heart*[1]

It's true to say that every step or leap forward in human understanding and knowledge is almost always the result of the originality and the hard-work-plus-imagination of a small group of individuals, usually starting with one. But, and this is as close to an axiom as can be, such breakthroughs are in turn dependent upon the insights and industry of hundreds of others, indeed often many thousands, over the years. Ecclesiastes was right. In a profound sense, "there is nothing new under the sun." Jon Kabat-

Zinn, who for many years has been the leading North American exponent of a fresh, unprecedented mind/body approach to stress reduction, is a prime example of this phenomenon. Head of The Stress Reduction Clinic at The University of Massachusetts for more than 20 years, Kabat-Zinn has put together a unique blend of Eastern and Western knowledge. In short, he has made a synthesis of over 2,500 years of Buddhist mindfulness meditation and hatha yoga on the one hand, and modern science, especially the leading edge of Behavioral Medicine, on the other. This may sound complex, but on closer inspection its essence is really fairly simple. The basic philosophy is one of wholeness in response to what Kabat-Zinn calls, following Zorba the Greek, "the full catastrophe" of life.[2]

In his books, *Full Catastrophe Living* and *Wherever You Go, There You Are*, the full program and the principles of the Massachusetts Clinic – now being widely followed at clinics and stress reduction centers in most major towns and cities continent-wide – are described in detail. For our purposes, a brief outline will be all that is needed.

"In these programs people learn to face their life problems and develop personalized strategies for working with them instead of giving themselves over to 'experts' who are supposed to just 'fix them' or make their problems magically disappear," writes Kabat-Zinn. "Such programs are vehicles in which people can work to become healthier and more resilient, in which they can change their beliefs about what they are capable of doing and learn to relax and cope more effectively with life stress." Part of this is helping people realize how changing their own lifestyles in "key ways" – how they think and how they deal emotionally with difficulties – can directly improve their health and overall sense of well-being. It's not just a matter of certain new disciplines; it's a matter of being assisted in expanding the way one sees oneself and his or her relationship to their own life and to the cosmos. The aim is to learn the *how* of taking care of oneself "not by replacing their medical treatment, but as a vitally important complement to it."[3]

The program itself, known as the Stress Reduction and Relaxation Program (SR&RP), is an eight-week course. The patients, who are referred by their doctors for a wide range of medical problems ranging from headaches, high blood pressure, back pain or heart disease, to cancer and AIDS, come hoping to regain some peace of mind and coping skills. They are of all ages and come from widely different backgrounds. Kabat-Zinn describes it as an "intensive, self-directed training program in the art of conscious living."

Just as in certain forms of Eastern martial arts you learn to use the strength, energy, and motion of an opponent to counter his or her attacks, so too in this approach. As we know, no pill, no doctor, no elixir can wholly ward off pain, suffering, or stress. So Kabat-Zinn's program is based upon helping you accept and learn "to work with the very stress and pain that is causing you to suffer." There are several aspects to this, with the key affirmation or underlying thrust being that there's always more right than there is wrong with you.

THE WAY OF AWARENESS

Buddhist teaching on "mindfulness" is at the root of this approach. Most of us go through life in a kind of trance, failing to live each moment or even realize that it's fleeting by. At the series of talks he once gave at Berkeley University, California, I remember how a bag of raisins was passed around. Each one of us had to take a raisin. First, we had to look at it from every angle as we felt its texture and shape; then we had to savor the scent or aroma fully; finally, we had to chew it slowly and lazily getting every nuance of flavor from it before finally swallowing it. It was only a simple beginning, but it made the simplest experience – eating a raisin – something rich, sensual, and alive. It became a sort of "eating meditation." At such a course, a lot of time each day is spent learning to be truly aware; aware of your body, your feelings, your fleeting and often very confused thoughts.

Though patients are taught to practice being really "awake" and aware every moment of the day, this new way of being is nurtured through the practice of daily periods (from 30 to 45 minutes if possible) of sitting quietly in a still place while breathing deeply in and out. Using the Buddhist technique of focusing completely on every breath as it goes in and then out through the nostrils – you can observe it lower down, entering and leaving the abdomen if you prefer – you learn to calm and quieten yourself. We all know how, in a tense situation, a few deep breaths can restore balance and equilibrium, at least to a degree. But in the yogic and Buddhist tradition, conscious breathing is the keystone of the arch.

"It is the very simplicity of the practice of mindfulness of breathing that gives it its power to disentangle us from the compulsive and habitual hold of the mind's many preoccupations," Kabat-Zinn says. "Yogis have known this for centuries. Breathing is the universal foundation for meditation practice."[4]

Just as all of nature pulsates with rhythms, the seasons, the ebb and flow of the tides, so also our bodies beat with circadian rhythms. These rhythms are connected to the rhythms of the planet in a continual interchange between our bodies and the planet of matter and energy. One fundamental life rhythm is the heartbeat. Another is the breath. The two working together create the pulse of life in us, and thereby the process under which we exchange matter and energy with the environment.

Although our breath is with us from the beginning to the end of our lives, we are not aware of it until something happens to prevent us from breathing normally. Or until we start to meditate.

During meditation, we pay so much attention to the breath because it is an obvious and convenient way of observing rhythm in our body, and thereby observing the change we can bring about.

It is normal for some people when very anxious to hyperventilate, which results in an increased loss of carbon dioxide and which can bring on lightheadedness, pressure in the chest, and panic. If you were to pass out from hyperventilation, your breathing would return to normal on its own. If the mind can be taught to work with the body's own wisdom before such a crisis is reached, much of the discomfort of anxiety can be eliminated.

Kabat-Zinn says that the breath "gives us stability, like the bridge piling anchored in bedrock as the river flows around it. Or, alternatively, it can remind us that ten or twenty feet below the surface of the ocean there is calmness."

Stress clinics that specialize in breathing techniques for controlling stress believe that breathing in a focused but relaxed way is the most important stress relieving mechanism that exists. They emphasize the importance of *being aware of* and *feeling* the breath, rather than controlling and thinking about it. Once the awareness is fully established, it becomes easier to connect the feelings of fear and anxiety with shallow, rapid breathing. A few deep abdominal breaths, called diaphragmatic breathing, can then start the process of deeper, slower breathing, which in turn will calm the body and the mind. If you've ever observed a baby sleeping, you've seen abdominal breathing, which is natural to infants, whom we hope have little worry and anxiety in their lives.

After years of chronic tension in our bodies, abdominal breathing must be relearned and practiced daily. But the reward is an inner peace that can make you feel you have come home to an old, familiar friend – one that perhaps you have not seen since young childhood.

The following is a simple exercise to try at the soonest appropriate moment:

1. Get comfortable, lying or sitting, with eyes closed or open, whichever feels right.
2. Breathe in deeply with your abdomen, as deeply as comfortably possible; then breathe out. Continue this process, imag-

ining you are a ship riding on large, slow waves, up and down, up and down...

3. When your mind wanders off, as it always will, observe what has taken your attention, then gently tell yourself you'll think about that later, after you're finished your exercise. If you have trouble concentrating, focus on the exhalation only, in the form of a sigh, which will take the pressure off the inhalation.

4. Do this for 15 minutes each day, enjoying the feeling that you don't have to do anything else for that time.

5. Throughout the day, whenever you think about your exercise, try to incorporate a few deep breaths as reminders.

THE BODY SCAN

In his courses, books, and tapes, Kabat-Zinn endlessly elaborates on this theme of waking up, watching the breath, and becoming more aware. For example, in the SR&RP clinic he teaches his patients how to scan their bodies as they learn to get out of their minds and to become more integrated by breathing into and out of every physical part. In caring for your body, he says, no matter if you are sick, well, or in between, step number one is to practice being "in" it.

HATHA YOGA AS MEDITATION

Many of us still tend to see hatha yoga (which consists of gentle stretches plus awareness of breathing) as a kind of self-torture in which the body is twisted into as many impossible positions as possible. That, of course, is silly. The word itself means "yoke" – as in the original Greek translation of the words of Jesus: Take my yoke (yoga) upon you – and refers to "realizing connectedness, realizing wholeness through disciplined practice."[5] At the stress clinic it's a matter of "yoking together" the body and mind. The great thing about hatha yoga is that it doesn't matter how old or young you are or – almost without limits – how incapacitated you may be. It can be done seated, standing, or lying down. The level and the amount you do are wholly relative to your wishes and situation.

To be personal for a moment. There was a time, long ago, that I scorned yoga as an activity for others perhaps, but not for me. In recent years particularly, I have come to awareness of just how ignorant of the truth I was. For several years now, I have been practicing a regular, first-thing-in-the-morning regimen that includes about 15 minutes of yoga together with a brief amalgam of some Qi Gong and Tai Chi exercises. I can only say that I wish I had begun it much earlier, in fact, in my youth, when I was playing English rugger and rowing instead. It's a great start to any day – even when the advance thought of it tempts me to sleep longer and forget it. I can also testify that what Kabat-Zinn teaches is correct. Done mindfully, with proper attention to the breath, it can bring relaxation, focus, and certainly far greater flexibility and agility than one would ever have without it. You become a better friend of your body; you sense body energy from its Source as never before. For Kabat-Zinn, as for millions around the world today, yoga is a form of meditation. It is a major weapon in his armament for stress reduction.

One can have nothing but the highest praise for these fresh, more holistic approaches to one of medicine's greatest challenges – increasing, chronic stress. Kabat-Zinn's books are filled both with colorful, anecdotal results, and with hard, scientific data on the evident effectiveness of his underlying philosophy, aims, and methods. One can get great benefit from reading and then re-reading his books. Yet there is a large piece of the puzzle still missing.

THE PARTIAL PARADIGM

With all due respect, the Kabat-Zinn model of "coming to wholeness" is, as hinted earlier, itself truncated or inadequate.

This becomes most glaring when he comes to the section of *Full Catastrophe Living* where he talks about encouraging his patients to have a "vision" of where their lives are intended to be going. Early on, he says: "to achieve peace of mind, people have to kindle a vision of what they really want for themselves and keep that vision in the face of inner and outer hardships, obstacles and setbacks."[6] This is at least the beginning of a more spiritual approach. But later on, when discussing his "new paradigm" more fully, the mind-body wholeness or connectedness to which he calls us, the "health" into which one is supposed to be growing seems disappointing, even ultimately nihilistic.[7] He quotes Albert Einstein on our need to escape from the delusions, thoughts, and feelings that make us feel separate from others and from the planet: "Our task must be to free ourselves from this prison by widening our circle of compassion to embrace all living creatures and the whole of nature in its beauty." But for Kabat-Zinn, it is seemingly enough to "perceive the intrinsic web of connectedness and merge with it."[8] This, he argues, is "healing." His vision, apparently, is that of pure Buddhism where one can observe "the ways in which we are each extraordinary and miraculous, without losing sight of the ways in which we are nothing special, just part of a larger whole unfolding, waves on the sea, rising up and falling back in brief moments we call life spans."[9] There are many who hold such a view and I have great appreciation of both their commitment and their quite often outstanding compassion. But the whole idea of one day being part of a cosmic wave sounding on an eternal shore, or of coming back out of that to possibly endless reincarnations (he doesn't say this explicitly, but it's what lies behind "coming back in brief moments we call life spans"), seems rather pointless to me and, no doubt, to many others. To my mind, he doesn't satisfactorily answer the question: what are we humans trying to be healthy for? That's a spiritual issue we'll return to in a moment.

IV

HEALTH FOR WHAT?

*Meditative practice is a wonderful way to reduce the overall stress
response to learn to stand back and not react so strongly in the world.
One of my favourite meditative guidelines captures the wonderful
humour and playfulness of meditative instruction.
It says one ought to practise meditation 30 minutes each day, unless
you have no time. Then 60 minutes is recommended.*

Dr. Barry Simon, a Toronto psychiatrist[1]

As I have learned over the years, there are many unforeseen
synchronicities which accompany the gestation and bringing to
birth of a book. There have certainly been many in the case of
Finding the Still Point. One in particular stands out at this juncture.
In July 2001, as I had just finished re-reading Kabat-Zinn's book
Wherever You Go, There You Are, I received a long letter in response
to one of my most recent columns in *The Toronto Sunday Star.*

The *Star* article was titled "On Making a Difference" and it
had reminded the author of the letter that he had once – after
hearing a lecture I had given at a church in Barrie, Ontario –
promised to write, in order to provide me with some information
about a mindfulness-based stress reduction program in which
he was involved. Included with his epistle were a number of

papers on different aspects of a Kabat-Zinn inspired Mindfulness-Based Stress Reduction program (MBSR), which is now part of the Barrie Community Health Centre's core services. Gary Machan, who wrote the letter, is the director of the center, it turned out. Barrie, Ontario, a fast-growing city of 100,000 (the population has doubled in the past ten years) is situated about one and a quarter hour's drive or train ride away from our home, about 60 miles north of Toronto, on the shores of beautiful Lake Simcoe. Thirty thousand people, almost a third of the total population, commute to jobs an hour or more away on the outskirts of the Greater Toronto Area (GTA). Most have young families and large mortgages. With both parents working, stress levels inevitably run high. So much to do, so little time.

Until Machan's letter, I had had no previous awareness of either the health center or its MBSR clinic. It happens to be one of several Kabat-Zinn spin-offs in southern Ontario; two more of them are in Toronto, one at the world-famous Princess Margaret Hospital, for cancer patients, and another at the Centre for Addiction and Mental Health. Incidentally, there are now over 250 such MBSR clinics based upon Kabat-Zinn's ideas in Canada, the United States, and internationally.

What interested me most about the letter was that Machan not only praised the MBSR techniques and their now-proven results, but also expressed some views about stress, panic, depression, and related ills that came very close to my own views.[2] He too was concerned about the general lack of a spiritual context in the now-popular MBSR program and other similar therapies. The cross-fertilization of ideas which ensued between us in the following correspondence, phone interviews, and then a couple of lengthy interviews face to face, including a visit to the health center, was to prove invaluable. In the letter, for example, from which the brief quotation was taken that leads into this chapter, he wondered aloud whether the mushrooming stress reduction clinics based upon deep-breathing, mindfulness, yoga, and meditation are not already "becoming the churches of the future." A provoking idea.

From my own reading and exposure to them, and the afore-mentioned group sessions with Kabat-Zinn himself in California, they *do* seem so much more relevant to where people are gen-uinely "at," so much more in touch with the pain, grief, and suffering that is all around us and within, but so often covered up or masked when formal religion is offered or approached. Having had several years' experience now with the Barrie Community Health Centre's (BCHC) eight-week stress reduction program, sometimes referred to as the "Still Point Program," and having seen well-documented successes there – in which significant reductions of problems such as daily stress loads, generalized anxiety, panic attacks, depression, and unbearable, daily pain were achieved – Machan nevertheless has some real concerns:

> *While being a strong proponent of mindfulness, the matter I have been struggling with most of late is that currently these programs are being offered in a purely secular manner; that is, the techniques (i.e., meditation, yoga, etc.) are sharply divorced from the religious traditions in which originally they were intricately interwoven over the past several millennia. To me, this is somewhat analogous to offering denuded white bread to the hungry versus the whole grain variety. You cannot help but lose something in the separation process.*

An example of Machan's point can be found in the way the yogic or Hindu traditions of physical and mental/emotional training, based as they are upon the breath and focusing on a mantra or sacred sound, have literally "swept the Western world." Yet they are historically only meant as *preparation* for union with the di-vine. Their intent is spiritual. The body is seen (as it is in Christian thinking) as the "temple" of God.[3] The Atman within is one with the great Atman over all things. Hindu women mark themselves with clay, for instance, as a witness to the belief that the "clay pot" of the body is the temple or dwelling of the divine. Hindus greet each other with a slight bow and a prayer-like bringing together of the hands. The intent is a salutation or recognition of the presence of God within the other.

Machan went on to make a comment that echoes much of my own thinking as I look at the problems of church and world, spirituality and secularity, and the current crisis for religion in general: "Moreover, this [omission of the spiritual context] is especially unfortunate because most of the religious traditions that I am familiar with are so steeped in wisdom that is perfectly compatible with what is being taught in stress reduction programs."

You can see why his letter rang such a bell. It was almost like listening to my own recent thinking – especially as he went on to argue that the impressive effectiveness of the Kabat-Zinn model and similar types of approaches "would nevertheless be further enhanced by offering the same techniques/program within the context of people's cultural/religio-spiritual heritage, rather than feed into the medical establishment's aversion to having anything to do with the forbidden 'S' [for spirituality] word." Machan dreams and plans, however, to set up a stress reduction program that does exactly this: it would expand the paradigm from body/mind to body/mind/spirit, as I'm proposing here. Like me, he believes a church, synagogue, temple, or mosque could be the natural and fitting place to begin.

I wanted to spend a little more time on this one local manifestation of the MBSR approach at the Barrie Community Health Centre for three reasons. First, because it is a very typical example of the spreading implementation of the Kabat-Zinn approach to stress. Second, because of its remarkable, overall leadership. Machan, together with psychologist Amy Moroz and psychiatrist Dr. Jack Reichmann, (Moroz and Reichmann actually run the MBSR clinic itself, while Machan is director of the entire health operation) are not just content to rest with the body/mind paradigm; they would like one day to push the envelope further to include the spiritual dimension more fully. But there is, of course, no preaching of any specific faith or spiritual approach in the Barrie clinic. Since they are publicly funded – the doctors' salaries and that of a midwife are paid by the Province of Ontario – they encourage patients and/or clients to find and nourish their own spirituality as they learn to look within, to know themselves better, and to draw on their inner strengths from the Source of all that is. The third reason for looking at all of this is that the ideas we're discussing precisely at this juncture provide a strong bridge to the rest of *Finding the Still Point* and its proposals.

Amy Moroz, who is a sparkling advertisement for the mindfulness way herself, holds a master's degree in clinical psychology, is a graduate of Kabat-Zinn's MBSR professional training program, and specializes in running meditation retreats and in psychological research.

Reichmann, M.D. FRCP (Canada), is a specialist in treating anxiety disorders using cognitive behavior therapy. He is director of the Centre for Stress and Anxiety in Barrie as well as being director of the anxiety clinic at the University of Toronto Health Network.

Reichmann, a family man who with his wife and two children lives in the woods north of Barrie, spends most of his time working with groups rather than seeing patients one-on-one in an office, as he used to do. In an interview, he said that the Barrie stress clinic program *does* include some spiritual content. "We have sessions where we ask people to be mindful for a while of their own spirituality – inviting them to meditate on such questions as who they really are, who is it that is experiencing everything, pain, panic attacks or whatever. That can have interesting results." But, at the same time, he said he didn't see either his role or the clinic's role as that of being an instrument to pressure people to go where they didn't want to go. What does he like most about the eight-week course? "The way it brings to distressed people a fuller awareness of what their experience is; the way it leads them away from avoidance of their suffering, by whatever means, into fully coming to grips with it." In short, he sees the course as giving people in pain the knowledge that they have the resources within themselves to manage their own problem in tandem with whatever modern medicine can do.

Here's one compact data report from among the many packed into Amy Moroz's bulging files. It's called "MBSR-BCHC Summer 2001, Brief Data Analysis and Summary," and contains a summary of the results of one of the Health Centre's recent stress reduction programs. After the eight-week course, using the Beck Anxiety Inventory as the criterion, there were statistically significant drops in the participating individuals' anxiety levels, their worry levels, and their fear levels. In relationships, they experienced a number of positive changes and, overall, they all were significantly less likely to report that their work was being negatively affected by their stress disorder.

For example, regarding anxiety levels, class "graduates" were significantly less likely to report the following symptoms "in the last several days":
- feeling tense, stressed, "uptight" or on edge
- difficulty concentrating
- racing thoughts
- skipping, racing, or pounding of the heart
- pain or tightness in the chest
- butterflies or discomfort in the stomach
- restlessness or jumpiness
- tight, tense muscles
- sweating not brought on by heat
- trembling or shaking.

WORRY QUESTIONNAIRE

A total of 12 out of 16 items listed revealed statistically significant, positive differences between pre- and post-test responses. In particular, individuals "were significantly less likely" to describe themselves in the following ways:

- Many situations make me worry;
- When I'm under pressure, I worry a lot;
- I'm always worrying about something;
- I worry all the time.

FEAR QUESTIONNAIRE

Individuals post MBSR program were "significantly less likely" to avoid a number of fear situations or feelings: for example, they were less likely to avoid hospitals, or situations where they might be watched or stared at, or opportunities for speaking or acting before an audience, and so on.

———

Stress…has reached epidemic proportions due to our fast-paced culture and, as a result, people are searching for solace wherever they can find it. The reality is that they are not finding it in churches, which appear to be far more interested in propping up old structures and inadvertently creating more stress in the process, than they are in responding to the needs of the people.

Gary Machan[4]

Gary Machan, 43, is married, with two children aged five and ten. His mother was a Holocaust survivor, but as a child and teenager he went to the Anglican (Episcopal) Church. He fell away for a time in his early 20s as he flirted with Buddhism, and then, influenced by the writings of modern, high-profile thinkers such as Creation theologian, Matthew Fox, and some of the ancient mystics, such as the German Dominican, Meister Eckhart (1260–1327), eventually came back to a liberal form of Christianity. Machan had joined the Royal Canadian Mounted Police at 19 but became increasingly aware of how police work in general deals with only the symptoms of much deeper social and psychosocial issues. He worked for a time with the Clarke Institute of Psychiatry, in Toronto, and then headed up a residence for delinquent teenagers in the Canadian North. Here he saw "kids coming in and making progress while being locked up." Then they were thrown out into society only to be flung back into correctional institutions again at varying rates of speed. To gain insight into what was really going on, he next went to college and got an M.A. in sociology, followed by a master's in social work. It was at that point that he was appointed director of the BCHC. Shortly after that, he saw the Bill Moyers PBS series called *Healing and the Mind* (Part three: Healing From Within). He was enthralled with the 30-minute segment on MBSR, featuring Jon Kabat-Zinn and his work. The seed had been sown. He determined that the Barrie Community Health Centre would become one of the first Canadian community clinics to run its own Kabat-Zinn based courses.

In our first interview, Machan said he loved his work, especially the MBSR program, its clients and its leadership, but that he was increasingly concerned with the kind of deeper issues already broached in his letter. Like myself, he feels "we Christians have short-changed Christianity; there's so much there we ignore. As a result, people move to other isms, martial arts, self-help gurus, or whatever. Often, they *do* learn stress response techniques, but lack any overall pattern, discipline, community, or tradition to keep them going on. Since there's no tradition or ethos or wider community for them, there's no ongoing support."

Machan, as noted, is part of the Christian community, specifically, The United Church of Canada, formed by a union of Presbyterians, Methodists, and Congregationalists back in 1925. But he has an ultra-ecumenical perspective. Since there are "no conflicts in silence," he sees mindfulness meditation fitting into any faith perspective from that of Christian Zen, to "High" Anglicanism, to Pentecostalism. It's about "paying attention," he says, about "living fully in the present moment," and about "compassion for all living things." All faiths can be comfortable with those principles and can connect with them in their own way.

Before moving to a description of spiritual meditation and some specific forms of it offered today, it's important to record a few other brief insights and comments Machan shared with me in our second meeting.

CAN SECULAR MEDITATION INCREASE STRESS?

Anyone who has seriously tried to meditate, using whatever method, for a fixed time period every day (even if only for a few weeks), can testify that it too can be quite stressful at first. When you "wake up" to the world, as meditation causes you to do, you become aware of aspects of your own life, or of the lives of others, that lay wholly unconscious before. The end result will be greater self-knowledge and sensitivity to a much wider world – a kind of transformation indeed – but the process, especially at first, can increase stress. As Machan puts it, "You then have to deal with what you've become aware of." (I should offer a caution at this point: Some experts warn that people who are seriously depressed should avoid meditation because it can encourage undue rumination. Please consult your own physician or therapist if you have this concern.)

NOT AN ALTERNATIVE NOR A PANACEA

People who are searching for a panacea, or hoping to make an "end run" around doctors, medicines, and professional Western science; or who are looking for an "alternative" to normal health care, should be warned that stress clinics à la Kabat-Zinn are not a substitute for anything else. "It can mean, perhaps, less medicine, or it can strengthen whatever the medical profession has to offer," Machan argues. But it is not designed to take its place.

SUFFERING AND PAIN AS TRANSFORMATIVE

Machan said that because our culture is so concerned about pain, distress, or discomfort of any kind, it's always important to remember a truth he has seen enacted many times: specifically, that while pain and suffering should always be treated to the full, they can have an extraordinary "transforming power" in people's lives, depending upon how they're viewed and responded to. This comment reminded me of the apostle Paul's famous statement, where he acknowledges his weaknesses and sufferings, and then admits that it has often been at these points of weakness that he has been made strong – just as God had declared to him, "My strength is made perfect in weakness."

I'm also reminded of some words of Father Laurence Freeman, OSB, director of the World Community for Christian Meditation. Commenting on the disastrous day of September 11, 2001, he said to me in an interview, "Whereas goodness never produces evil, evil frequently leads to good."[5]

There are a few beautiful and highly relevant lines that come to mind from some writing by May Sarton. The poem is called "Invocation to Kali," the Hindu name for the divine power of destruction and upheaval in nature and in human life:

> Help us to be the always hopeful
> Gardeners of the spirit
> Who know that without darkness
> Nothing comes to birth,
> As without light
> Nothing flowers.[6]

A SPIRITUAL CONTEXT

Ultimately, there has to be a spiritual context for any of the responses to stress to truly "work," to touch the depths of our being and give a framework or grounding for everything else. Machan is convinced of this and so am I. It's not enough to do everything we can from a purely secular point of view. Ultimately, we have to ask the question, "Health for what?" If there is no final meaning or purpose for human living beyond merging back into the cosmic mix, what is all the health-driven striving and effort and expense about? What is the point? In particular, why bother to meditate anyway? This is where our investigation takes us next.

PART TWO

THE
SPIRITUAL
RESPONSE

V

SPIRITUAL MEDITATION

There are times ... when in order to keep ourselves in existence at all we simply have to sit back for a while and do nothing. And for a man [sic] who has let himself be drawn completely out of himself by his activity, nothing is more difficult than to sit sill and rest, doing nothing at all. The very act of resting is the hardest and most courageous act he can perform: and often it is quite beyond his power. We must first recover the possession of our own being before we can act wisely or taste any experience in its human reality. As long as we are not in our own possession, all our activity is futile. If we let the wine run out of the barrel and down the street, how will our thirst be quenched?

Thomas Merton, *No Man Is an Island*[1]

INTRODUCTION

Before looking at spiritual meditation in general, this is a fitting point at which to say something about the fundamental nature of human beings. We can't talk meaningfully or long about any aspect of human life without facing the need for an agreed-upon, rational understanding of who we are and where we come from. It makes a tremendous amount of difference whether or not we are simply "alone and afraid in a world we never made"; creatures of fate, adrift in an accidental universe with no purpose, calling, or final destiny. Were such to be truly the case, there would be little point in anything. Atheists, existentialists, and the fiercer brand of agnostics or sceptics may deny this, but nihilism and despair lie at the end of their logic. Many today not necessarily given to abstract thinking or philosophizing about their lives nevertheless witness to the angst and the longing or to the feelings of sheer emptiness that lurk within. Much of the frantic busyness – for the sake of busyness, or its opposite, the torpor that engulfs so many as they mindlessly watch TV or compulsively overeat, over-buy, or cater to a range of other addictions – bears eloquent witness to this.

If, on the other hand, the once-predominant religious vision is correct – that we have the divine Mystery whom we call God as our beginning, our sustainer, and our end – then the whole picture changes. This is where Christianity in particular, (like Judaism and also Islam) has taken a very firm stand.

This doesn't mean, of course, that you have to accept somebody else's literalist version of the story of creation or of any other part of scripture to comprehend its essential meaning and significance – thank God.

One of the best-known classical art works in the Western world, Michelangelo's "The Creation of Adam," painted on the ceiling of the Vatican's Sistine Chapel (1508–1512 CE), expresses this "true myth" of divine creation uniquely. The symbolic portrayal of God reaching out from above to give Adam the divine touch that brings him to life is immensely powerful. The late Father Arthur Gibson – an old Basilian priest friend of mine, who taught at St. Michael's College, Toronto, for many years – never tired of pointing out to his students the important fact that the artist has left a significant gap between the fingers of Adam and the finger of God. They don't actually touch. There is a space between the two hands signifying that while Adam is a created being, he is free.

There is something else that is much less remarked upon. Michelangelo's imaginative rendering of the creation of humanity differs somewhat from the biblical text itself. Many of you will know that there are two accounts of this mythic event which have been put in the Genesis text one after the other. The first one (Genesis 1:1 – 2:4) says this, at verse 26:

> *And God said, let us make man in our image, after our likeness: and let them have dominion...So God created man in his own image, in the image of God created he him; male and female created he them.*
>
> [Note that male and female, in this version, were created simultaneously.]

The second version (Genesis 2:4–25) states this in verse 7:

> *And the Lord God formed man out of the dust of the ground, and he breathed into his nostrils the breath of life; and man became a living soul.*
>
> [Both passages are taken from the KJV.]

In this version it is the breath of God that gives Adam (humans) life and the power to become a living soul. We observe that here Eve was created separately and later. As professor Gibson regularly pointed out, according to the Bible, we don't have or possess souls – like hands or an appendix – we have *become* souls by an act of God's breath or Spirit.

Steeped in a scientific worldview or offended by the word "myth," many make the serious mistake of passing over these two accounts as though irrelevant or fairy-tale in nature. But when Bible scholars use the term myth, they are saying that these particular stories contain truths so profoundly spiritual they can only be conveyed through or by a story. They're beyond mere history or science. Together, these two stories clearly state that we are not just a randomized result of blind processes, the products of a cosmic lottery, but that we are truly "God-sourced" spiritual beings. We are created by God and are intended to live in and for God. We are made in God's very likeness and image – not physically of course, but spiritually. There is, to use another metaphor, a "God-shaped space" at our core.

It's this dimension of Christian, Jewish, Muslim, Hindu and other religious anthropologies, that makes them so different from the mechanistic anthropology underlying mainline secular spiritualities. It's a difference to which we shall return in due course.

SPIRITUAL MEDITATION

Many years ago, the controversial Roman Catholic theologian, author, and critic of the church, Hans Küng, came to Oxford to deliver a lecture. It was during a brief break in the Second Vatican Council (1962–1965), where Küng was acting as one of the Periti, (experts) appointed by Pope John XXIII himself. The precise date was the spring of 1963. I happened to be back at my old college, Oriel, for some post-graduate studies and so had the opportunity to hear him speak. His subject was "The Roman Catholic Church and Freedom." I still remember his opening remarks. One of his more secular friends in Rome, he said, had asked him what he would be talking about up in Oxford. When he heard the topic, the associate said gently, with a smile, "The Roman Catholic Church I know, and freedom I know. But the Roman Catholic Church *and* freedom, what's that?" The Catholic professors, clergy, and students in the hall laughed the loudest.

That moment of innocent, humorous relief came to my recall as I wrote the words "Spiritual Meditation" at the head of this chapter. Many will possibly be thinking "Spirituality I know and meditation I also know. But spiritual meditation, what's that?"

Put at its briefest, spiritual meditation is everything that is conveyed by the word meditation – the techniques or methods can be identical – but seen from or practiced from the perspective described in the prelude above. That is to say, its roots and its goals, its ethos and its principles, flow from the conviction that we are spirit-mind-body beings, sustained by and living in the presence of our Divine Source. In God, we are one family with all other humans, with all other life, and with the whole of the cosmos itself. Hindus, Christians, Sikhs, Muslims, Jews, Baha'is, native spiritualities – every faith tradition, even strict Buddhism, when one gets past certain difficulties raised chiefly by semantics I'm convinced, believe in this well-nigh universal "philosophy."

A DIMENSION FOR EXPLORATION –
THE "PROBLEM" OF GOD

The mysterious reality most of us intend to refer to or address when we speak the divine name – and all the synonymous terms, from Allah to Yahweh or Brahman to Om – cannot, by definition or logic, be defined. Any attempt to confine Ultimacy, the great mystery that both shakes us with awe and at the same time eternally rivets our hearts and spirits in fascination (*mysterium tremendum et fascinosum*); any attempt to restrict the He/She or That "whom the heaven of heavens cannot contain" to a creed, or a formula, or a learned proposition is doomed to create a blasphemous idol. What the most devout as well as the more casual "believer" must never forget is that all religious claims and assertions regarding God inevitably tend towards putting God in a box or straitjacket.

That's why all religious language about deity is bound to be metaphorical – and at best a "limping metaphor," not one that strides! That's the point of a poem by C. S. Lewis hitherto unknown to me until I came across it not long ago. He is writing here about prayer but for the same reasons:

He whom I bow to only knows to whom I bow
When I attempt the ineffable Name, murmuring Thou,

He whom I bow to only knows to whom I bow
When I attempt the ineffable Name, murmuring Thou,
And, dream of Phidian fancies and embrace in heart
Symbols (I know) which cannot be the thing Thou art.
Thus always, taken at their word, all prayers blaspheme
Worshipping with frail images a folk-lore dream,
And all men in their praying, self-deceived, address
The coinage of their own unquiet thoughts, unless
Thou in magnetic mercy to Thyself divert
Our arrows, aimed unskilfully, beyond desert;
And all men are idolaters, crying unheard
To a deaf idol, if Thou take them at their word.
Take not, Oh Lord, our literal sense, Lord, in Thy great
Unbroken speech our limping metaphor translate.

Oxford Book of Prayer[2]

[Note: Phidias was the best-known sculptor of Athens in the 5th century BCE.]

In my own praying, I try from time to time to acknowledge the truth Lewis describes so well by using my own words, "O God, I pray to You, not as I imagine or suppose You are, but as You know Yourself to be." I encourage you to find your own way of meeting this possible stumbling block, or feel free to use something like what I've just described. One thing has become most apparent to me over my lifetime so far; very often when a self-styled sceptic, agnostic, or even atheist talks honestly about the reasons for declining any invitation to believe or trust in God, what they usually describe are the off-putting, anti-reason, anti-faith statements and arguments of doctrinaire "religious" people. The arrogant assurance that one group or other has a "corner on God," or the only valid understanding of divine truth, is more than enough to frighten off or flood with laughter anyone with a capacity to reflect intelligently. The truth is that once you get past the negative experiences of bad religion such people have had, you find they are often much "closer to the Kingdom of God" than those whose protestations of belief are frequently the loudest.

To involve oneself in spiritual meditation does *not* mean joining or sharing in my views and opinions about God, nor in anyone else's for that matter. But it *does* mean coming to terms with the belief that we are indeed spiritual beings, that there is Spirit, or a Spirit, and that our very being comes from and returns to that Wellspring of all Life. To call oneself "spiritual" or a seeker after "spirituality" and yet to deny that foundation, is, I'm convinced, the real reason why so much would-be spirituality today – however chic and popular – is actually devoid of energy and ultimate meaning. One is reminded of the words of the apostle Paul, when he admonished those in the early church who were putting on a "show of godliness" while at the same time "denying the Power of it."

A LONG TRADITION

I have been surprised in my reading as well as in visiting congregations of various churches in England, Canada, and the USA, at the way in which spiritual meditation or sacred meditation as some call it is still avoided like the proverbial plague, as if it were some kind of New Age or New Wave invention. This is especially true of the more evangelical wing of the churches, or the so-called conservatives, but it is true of the mainline, middle-of-the-road strata in every denomination as well. It's not just the absence of times of silence for meditation, either directed or undirected, during worship services; it's the complete absence of any training or study devoted to meditation at all. Thus, a remarkable opportunity for communication, relevancy, and actual healing is left begging entirely. This is a matter we will return to, but it's important to point out at this juncture because this neglect goes directly against the most ancient traditions of the Christian faith.

When the gospels inform us that Jesus sometimes spent whole nights in prayer, never mind the 40 days in the wilderness before the outset of his ministry, we would be foolish to suppose that this whole time was spent in verbal petitions, supplications, or the like. Similarly, when Paul spent three years in Arabia just after his conversion and before launching his missionary journeys, some of these many hours were undoubtedly spent either meditating on the Word (the Old Testament, the only Bible he had) or simply meditating, period. We know that all the great Christians of the earliest days of the church spent long hours in meditation as a regular part of their overall spirituality. Take, for example, the Desert Monks of the second, third, and fourth centuries CE. The monastic movement began in Egypt but spread to the west during the fourth century and, of course, has survived into this new millennium. St. John Chrysostom, a favorite Church Father of mine (c.347–407CE) who eventually became Bishop of Constantinople, at one time spent three years in a cave, praying and meditating, and is said to have committed to memory the entire Bible, both Testaments.

Such Christian meditation was sometimes mantra-based (though the term itself was not used, belonging as it does to much older traditions among the Hindus). This is evidenced by the very ancient Jesus Prayer or mantra still used in the Orthodox churches of the East: "Jesus, Son of God, have mercy upon me a sinner."

The idea for monks especially was to continuously repeat this, softly or inwardly, in rhythm with the breath, whether at work, in conversation, or wherever. The name of Jesus by itself was a sacred mantra and the Aramaic phrase Maranatha ("Come Lord," or "the Lord has come"), of which more will be said shortly, was widely in use from earliest times as well. The later mystics, such as Meister Eckhart, Julian of Norwich, Teresa of Avila, and many others, practiced various versions of meditation daily. This tradition has continued here and there, especially in cloistered communities, to the present day. As for the church in general, as Chrysostom said, meditation was one of the "jewels" that was largely lost. The important point to reiterate here, however, is that sacred meditation belongs not to the periphery of

Christian faith, worship, and daily practice but to its very ancient center. It is there waiting to be possessed again.

UNDERMINED BY THE PREVAILING ZEITGEIST AND WORLDVIEW

As far as we can discern,
the sole purpose of human existence is to kindle a light
in the darkness of mere being.

C. G. Jung[3]

The prevailing "spirit of the times" and a popular, culturally shared worldview powerfully influence how we "see" everything in our lives.

The chief problem with this phenomenon is that, for most people, this influence, this shaper of all our opinions, is virtually 100 percent unconscious. We go about like people who wear sunglasses all the time. We may be aware at first that we're viewing everything through colored lenses. But imperceptibly, we become so accustomed to our ultimately distorting manner of sight that we forget and ignore what's conditioning our entire outlook.

Today, the great majority of us walk about in a sort of cultural trance. We seldom if ever stop long enough to examine our "glasses," our basic presuppositions and secular dogmas.[4] The one which is the most potent of all, and the least challenged, is our assumption that only what can be empirically proven can be true. In other words, we take it for granted that only what belongs to the world of science is a part of real knowledge. All reality, it is thus assumed, must be capable of a scientific explanation, must be the product of scientific logic and experimentation. Everything else is automatically suspect. Never mind that this assumption is really not in itself scientific. It is properly called a part of "scientism," which is bogus science. For example, the proposition that only science gives one true knowledge is not provable by scientific reasoning. It must be taken on faith alone, thus standing Martin Luther's *sola fide*, salvation solely by faith, completely on its head!

Thinkers such as Matthew Fox, Thomas Berry, Brian Swimme, and a host of others, have identified today what they call "The New Story of Science," which includes quantum physics, "Big Bang" cosmology, and cosmogony (the former deals with the overall story of the universe, the latter focuses on its origins). This "New Story of Science" has changed the old scientific thinking, with its distorted step-child scientism, completely. For example, the thinking in physics at this moment points directly to the probability that mysticism, meditation, and other more non-linear ways of perceiving reality bring insights just as clear or even brighter than pure left-brain thinking by itself.[5]

Thus, for example, the very ancient "meditation of Eastern religions" on life and the cosmos, which is deeply spiritual, commands as much authority in many minds now as the Western "meditation" on reality (i.e., science).

Both are necessary for the whole truth.

Nevertheless, the old trance, the now-outdated "glasses" of scientism are still firmly in place for most. As a result, any mention of meditation falls on most ears as talk of an alien, suspect activity. It's assumed that if it isn't lightweight hocus-pocus of some kind, then it must be sinister. I have already mentioned this above in the context of religious suspicion, but I want to underline it strongly in this wider, secular setting. To make this error is to miss a great treasure, something I and many like me profoundly wish had been taught and practiced in the families and academic institutions which shaped us long ago.

METHODS AND APPROACHES

In *Prayer: The Hidden Fire*, I wrote personally, but briefly, about spiritual meditation. Much, however, has changed in the world at large and in all of our lives since 1998. For myself, I had not yet at that time had very much experience with meditation, especially as it bears on the central issue before us now – anxiety, worry, nervousness, panic, and all the other physical, mental, and emotional symptoms that stress throws up. It's not that there was no stress before, of course, since life as we've concluded seems to afford us all plenty of that. Also, I had been practicing meditation, although fairly casually as I see now, for some time. But various pressures, common to all but singularly poignant nevertheless to each of us, then intervened. For example, my mother died on December 2, 1997, on the eve of her 90th birthday, just after my last book was completed but was as yet unpublished; my wife, Susan, lost her mother five weeks later after a very lengthy illness, on January 8, 1998, and her father died on April 9, 1999 – all three of them within a space of 16 months, together with two or three other close relatives on Susan's side of the family. On top of that, we moved twice in the almost three years overlapping these events, the first move coming right in the middle of all the promotional, across-Canada travel and interviews the book on prayer involved. At the same time, I struggled to keep up with a steady workload of public appearances plus regular column writing for *The Toronto Sunday Star*. That's not all by any means, yet I assure you that we feel we have been brought even closer to each other and to the Divine through it all. My purpose here is just to create the context that necessitated bringing meditation, silence, and solitude into a much more disciplined and serious interface with the growing stress in our own lives. It also threw light on and drew our attention to the much greater stress in so many other people's lives at this epochal moment of history. In short, we learned a lot.

Specifically, I was forced to realize that in addition to learning to say "no" more firmly, I urgently needed to find a way or ways of coping more effectively with tension and stress in general. Notice, I am talking here of coping with or responding to stress, not of "beating stress," overcoming it, or, faint hope, of "eliminating" it from one's life. One can perhaps through a va-

riety of strategies, from wholly evading responsibilities and opportunities for service to others, to giving in to a smorgasbord
of addictions and/or a range of distractions, evade some of life's
stress. But at what price? That route, as we all know, is not really
fulfilling in the end.

So I intensified some of the various approaches I was already making part of my "spiritual practice" – such as daily
meditating while walking, and using a variety of prayers and
mantras at odd times throughout the day as the spirit moved me.
But, most importantly for me, was the decision to dedicate the
time at the beginning of every day – the period between rising
and sitting down to breakfast – to 20 minutes of exercise (a self-
styled mix of hatha yoga, Tai Chi and Qi Gong), plus 10 to 20
minutes of meditation proper. I have written elsewhere of a lifelong discomfort with any religious or spiritual regime, of whatever kind, for the earliest hours of morning. It seemed to me
there were two kinds of people: those who got something out
of the daybreak stuff and those who didn't. That assumption was
the one I most needed to challenge.

What I have found is that for all these years I was getting by
(or trying to) with a rather flimsy excuse for avoiding what I
had always suspected might be best, if only I could find the
fortitude to try it. I have tried the first-thing-in-the-morning
routine for over three years now and I find increasingly that,
while it still has a few of its painful aspects, the meditation experts are right after all. If you do it right away, it's there as a
foundation for the entire day. If you put it off until later, the risk
of missing it altogether is simply too great.

Truly, I have come now to anticipate and welcome being in
my study by close to 7:00 a.m., doing the exercise and meditation while listening to some quiet, reflective music, or while
silently watching the wild birds at the feeder outside the window. I have gradually (it seems miraculously) come to experience it as the best, most alert and energy-filled time of the whole

24-hour cycle. The methods I use still vary for the meditation part. They range from simple sitting meditation (sometimes sitting cross-legged on the floor which I find to be somehow more empowering or grounding – at least until it becomes uncomfortable or a cramp sets in!), to lying on my back for a total body-scan. Sometimes I inwardly say a mantra, such as the Hebrew word *shalom* (meaning peace). At others times, I employ a visualization of one kind or another. The key thing is that it be a time of being silent in God's presence.

The variety is important, I've found, but many others, millions in fact, find it is more effective for them to use a habitual sacred mantra, such as Amen, Shalom, Peace, One, or a line from a favorite psalm or some other passage from one of the world's traditional scriptures.

What makes all this, the exercise and the meditation, sacred or spiritual? In so many ways it resembles the kind of secular, non-religious meditation described in Part One of this book. Well, it's partly the intention – not to ask for anything or even expect anything, but simply to draw closer to God or Divine Spirit, to open your being steadily and repeatedly to the Light that is behind all lesser lights. You can do this either by a brief visualization of the Light coming to surround and fill yourself, or even more simply by silently invoking the Divine Presence at the start. The source of the mantra, if one is being used, plays a part in making this a matter of the Spirit, and hence spiritual. So, of course, does the meditator's underlying belief in and desire to know better the Author and Sustainer of his or her total person, and of all beings. Sometimes, a specifically sacred object, such as a cross (I have a small brass Celtic cross from Ireland on my study wall above the arched window), a lit candle, an icon, a sculptured Buddha, a mandala, or a symbol of Brahman, can be useful in focusing one's attention, according to one's own belief system.

The bottom line for me is that whatever flexibility one introduces into such a morning practice, I have finally found in my own experience that the regular discipline of at least six early morning sessions a week does indeed make a vital difference to how I respond to stress. This is true for my general levels of anxiety in what we have already referred to as "the full catastrophe" of life in this world, as well as to the amount of angst, with concomitant symptoms, I have always known when engaged in public speaking, media interviews, or when meeting crucial deadlines. A certain tingling of the nerves and a feeling of "butterflies" in the stomach or abdomen, as most performers in politics, the arts, or sports are well aware, is necessary for peak activity. But too much adrenaline can cause one to "choke" or at least do less than one's best. It's a fuel that could stoke the fires of burnout.

VI

THE WORLD COMMUNITY FOR CHRISTIAN MEDITATION

Let us not look back at the past, in anger.
Let us not look ahead to the future, in fear.
Let us look around us in the present, and be aware.
James Thurber

This book is meant for people of all the various major religions as well as for those who have no faith denomination or creed whatsoever – a fast-growing company these days. There is only one God, but there are many ways of knowing God. Still, I write from a Christian perspective myself and realize that most of the readers in this case will be either inactive, borderline, "underground," searching, or active Christians. Since the majority of Christians generally, keen and not-so-keen, still have today, in my experience, a markedly biased outlook on meditation – in most cases based upon a distorted understanding of what it's all about – it's important, I believe, to give wider exposure to an expanding worldwide movement aimed particularly, though not solely, at them (us).

The World Community for Christian Meditation (WCCM), headquartered in London, England, has scores of groups or local chapters in most major cities of the English-speaking world. For example, there are about 30 such groups in the Greater Toronto Area in southern Ontario alone, with a total of about 200 across Canada, from the Maritime provinces to the Yukon Territory. Quebec has about 40 groups. Brisbane, Australia, has an impressive 60 chapters. Similar chapters meet in New York, Oxford, Florida, Texas, Brazil, Northern Ireland, Italy, Holland – the list is almost endless. Members meditate daily and meet to hear speakers, do communal meditation, and socialize regularly in either weekly or monthly gatherings. Once a year, there is a John Main Seminar (so-named after the founder), in some major center – in the fall of 2000, it was in Belfast, Northern Ireland; in 2001, in Brisbane; and in the summer of 2002, Cornwall, Ontario. Each year the seminar is built around some major theme of global interest.

The WCCM was founded by an English/Irish Benedictine monk, Dom John Main, OSB (1926–1982) in 1975. He was a monk who knew this world well. Before becoming a Benedictine, he had been a journalist, a soldier, and a barrister who taught law at Trinity College, Dublin, for four years upon graduating. In the summer of 1974, after a five-year assignment in Washington, D.C., he was recalled by his abbot to Ealing Abbey, in London. Something very significant for his future, however, had occurred while he was still in the United States. He had discovered a book, *Holy Wisdom*, by a Benedictine monk, Augustine Baker. The volume was an edition of the writings of a fourth-century desert monk by the name of John Cassian. In his words about prayer, Cassian discusses the value of repeating inwardly a brief biblical verse or phrase in helping bring about interior silence. Cassian strongly recommended this "saving formula" as the best way to counter mental and emotional distractions and to direct one to inner stillness and peace. Main was later to discover that this same practice is recommended in a famous English treatise of the 14th century, *The Cloud of Unknowing*, and in some other ancient books on contemplation and prayer.

Paul T. Harris, of Ontario, describes all of this in a "25 Year Retrospective" in a special January 2000 issue of the WCCM's *Christian Meditation* newsletter/magazine. Harris says that, for Main, discovering Cassian's teaching was "a great breakthrough" because Main had already discovered the practice of repeating a mantra or sacred phrase about 20 years earlier. At that time, however, he had learned it from a Hindu swami in Malaya. "Overjoyed at learning that this way of prayer was rooted in the practice of the early Christian desert monks also, Main received permission from the abbot to establish a small lay community on the monastery grounds at Ealing that would be dedicated to what Father John referred to as the practice of Christian Meditation," Harris writes.

By the autumn of 1975, four young men had come and joined the lay community, including Laurence Freeman who himself later became a Benedictine monk and who is today the world leader of the WCCM. Another of the four was Tom Abraham, who came from India his home, to Ethiopia, to Ghana, and at last to London, where he was working on a Ph.D. degree in electrical engineering at Imperial College. Abraham had heard about Christian meditation from a friend and he was determined to meet Fr. John. His description of his first impressions of Main is well-worth repeating here since I think it gives more of the "flavor" of Main's personality than is found in the several other books that have been written about him.

> In December, 1975, I finally got an opportunity to meet Father John at the lay community centre in Ealing. I must admit that I had conjured up an image of this priest as young, inexperienced, and probably into meditation as a fad, as the "thing to do" in the

1970s. On that particular evening I had just placed
one foot in the meditation room when a firm, strong
voice behind me said, "We take off our shoes when
we go into the meditation room." So much for my
preconceived image of Father John. Here was a ma-
ture monk who, I subsequently learned, had been
meditating for twenty years. He had an impeccable
English accent and an imposing personality. When he
began to speak about meditation it was with authority and assurance and no pussyfooting around. His
message was quite clear and straightforward. This was
the teacher I had been looking for.

At our evening recreation in the lay community
house, Father John would often join us and entertain
us with hilarious stories and mimicry. He had a gift of
accents and could imitate…a variety of dialects. Up
to this point we had two meditations a day, morning
and evening. Then one day I accidentally discovered
John and Brother Laurence meditating at noon. This
was another aspect of Father John's character. He never
put any pressure on anyone in regard to meditation.
No persuasion or arm-twisting. He always hoped you
would on your own accord join in. Needless to say,
we all freely and joyfully joined in this third daily
meditation.

Many other people came to join this first meditation group started at Ealing, including Lady Lovat,
wife of the war-hero, Lord Lovat. Another person at-
tracted was a Sacred Heart nun, Madeleine Simon.
She recalls that one evening she had only intended to
drop off a sister of her congregation at Ealing Abbey
and return home. However, a tall, black-habited figure on the doorstep (John Main) invited her in and
she found herself in her winter boots in a room full of

silent people."By the time I left," says Sister Madeleine, "I was saying to myself, this is for me." Sister Madeleine went on to found, a few years later, a Christian Meditation Centre in the Kensington area of London.

Sister Madeleine also recalled a meeting with John Main a couple of years later, spring in 1982, in Montreal: "It was at this time, too, that I discussed with him the possibility of my opening a co-ordinating centre for his work in England. I suggested 'Christian Meditation Centre' as a name for it. He thought for some time and then said, 'Yes, that says just what it should be, and I hope that, in due course, there will be Christian Meditation Centres all over the world.'"[1]

Today there are over 2,000 groups, 30 meditation centers, and many thousands of members in 60 countries around the globe.

THE NATURE OF FATHER MAIN'S "CHRISTIAN MEDITATION"

Meditation is our way to being fully human, fully alive. We are all called to this. To meditate is to be in the centre of ourselves and of all reality and to be conscious that the centre is not ourselves but God. This is why meditation changes people and the world in which they live.

John Main

John Main spent the last five years of his life running a small urban monastic community in Montreal devoted to WCCM-style traditions and teaching, in particular, the sharing of the practice of meditation in the Christian manner of desert father John Cassian. But, what exactly was that?

First of all, it shares many of the characteristics of what I have elsewhere called "secular" meditation:

1. It takes place in a room or special place in one's home dedicated to being still, a silent place. It may or may not involve having a candle to light. Certainly it will be private and available at the same time each day for morning and possibly evening sessions of from 10 minutes to 30 or 40 minutes. (It's best to begin with about 10 minutes and gradually work up to at least 15 or 20 minutes.)

2. One sits on an upright chair, back straight, head erect, feet flat on the floor, and hands on each knee lightly, or clasped – cupping the right hand in the left – in one's lap. Vary all this slightly to suit your own comfort, but try to find a position that has dignity. You are claiming your inheritance as a child of God, a carrier and channel of divine light.

3. You focus your awareness on your breath going steadily and deeply in and out through the nose. You feel your chair solidly beneath you, the grounding energy of the floor beneath your feet. You are still, and in the silence slowly begin to repeat within yourself the word *Maranatha*. Maranatha is an Aramaic word – the language widely believed by scholars to have been the tongue spoken by the disciples of Jesus and Jesus himself. Maranatha occurs in the pages of the New Testament. For example, in 1 Corinthians 16:22. The original Greek text has Maranatha, printed as two words: Marana Tha. It means either "Our Lord has come," or, more likely, in prayer form, the imperative, "O Lord, come" as in Revelation 22:20, where the author closes his strange book with these words (in Greek): "He who witnesses to these things says: 'Indeed, I am coming swiftly.' Amen. Come, Lord Jesus."

Neither John Main nor the WCCM have laid it down in fixed terms that this Aramaic phrase, used by Cassian and others from earliest church history, is absolutely essential. One could use the term "amen" as I have suggested elsewhere; or "shalom," the Hebrew word for peace with justice and right relations; or any sacred word(s) of special meaning and sacredness for you. They do, however, strongly recommend Maranatha because of the fact that it has very few thought-patterns or associations for the average person and so the act of simply focusing on it can be less cerebral or "thinking" orientated. The object of the exercise, at one level, is to divert the mind's chattering-to-itself by means of the mantra so that one can enjoy the silence of pure being and pure consciousness in the presence of God.

Father Laurence Freeman, the successor of Main and his tradition of Christian meditation, travels the globe carrying the Maranatha message and founding new chapters. From numerous tapes of his, together with hearing and meeting him at the Belfast Seminar in October 2000 (where he was in dialogue with the Dalai Lama) and then interviewing him for this book as well as for my columns, I feel I know him really well. He emphasizes something I have found increasingly to be so in my own life since first beginning spiritual meditation several years ago. The constant inner repetition of a sacred mantra of one's choice, "in season and out of season," through dry spells and through times of joy, brings an ever-deepening awareness of creative harmony building within; a capacity to be at peace with oneself, with others, and with all aspects of creation. This becomes increasingly so as the weeks go by and the mantra comes almost automatically so that one can focus more on "the poverty and simplicity of silence."

Freeman speaks of the word for "sin" in our day being not sin itself, but alienation. Young people, for example, may not actually use the word alienation either but the adjectives they *do* use to describe their innermost feelings, and especially the lyrics of their favorite songs, are really partial or full definitions of alienation. They talk at times of overwhelming ennui or boredom; they speak of a kind of cosmic "loneliness," and of feeling what can best be described as *taedium mundi* or world-weariness. All too often, their life seems to them to be void of meaning and purpose beyond the instant pleasures of sex, or other "highs" and "rushes" provided by alcohol, various drugs, or rebellion in a range of activities sometimes legal but often not. Their music reveals it all most eloquently.

According to Freeman, following Main, with habitual meditation, the realization that God is not only all around us but also within us takes hold in the depths of our inner selves – our often deeply divided selves – and gradually forges a wholeness and integration. As the Buddhists say, "The mind must be the key to the heart." So, in Freeman's words, Christian meditation begins with the mind, as it accepts the idea and the discipline involved, but it soon leads to a growing unity of mind and heart together. It ends with the heart, the place out of which flows the very source of ourselves – God's indwelling Presence, the Spirit, or Atman, to use the Hindu word.

Like Jon Kabat-Zinn and other secular meditation gurus, the Main/Freeman teaching says to try as much as possible to put all expectations aside and to just "be" where you are as the mantra is quietly recited.

The following are the only rules for Christian meditation.

1. Say the mantra over and over again until all the allotted time (say 20 minutes) has been used up.
2. Don't make haste; don't force anything.
3. Don't let anything that happens – phones ringing; knocks at the main door; sudden, unexpected street or other noises; fits of coughing or itching, etc. – distract you from "the work."
4. As far as you can, allow yourself to go beyond thought, beyond imagination, far past all mental images in order to rest in the realized presence of the "Ground of all Being," God, in your heart. Don't strain. Relax, and don't judge if that takes time. Let it be. "Learn to rest in the infinity of God," in boundless love, in limitless compassion, in eternal joy and life without limit. I am reminded of William Blake's famous words: "If

the doors of perception were cleansed, every thing would appear to man as it is: infinite. For man has closed himself up, till he sees all things thro' narrow chinks of his cavern." Freeman believes that once we see who we truly are in the light of what God truly is, the total transformation of our true, innermost selves begins. As Paul says, this is "through the power of God which works within us."

Such daily meditation can be the opportunity to shrug off all the false images that we hold of ourselves – as weak or as ultrastrong, as totally destined to an outlook of perpetual fear, nervousness and angst, or to depression – and to see again what we really have been made to be: alert, aware, calm, and bearers of the light within, channels of God's purposes in the world. Christian Meditation affirms this light and life in each of us. As Freeman has said: "It makes us know our divine nature and how infinitely holy we are. It was said of St. Benedict, the founder of religious orders, "He dwelleth within himself." That is to say, the monk had achieved the enlightenment of waking up to whom in God's sight he truly was. To quote St. Irenaeus, he had discovered for himself that "The glory of God is man [the human], fully alive." Learning to pray or meditate in this manner, Freeman says, is to live as fully as possible "into the now," committed to the present moment with no thought for the past, ours or others', and no thought for the future, ours or others'. This inner pilgrimage, a pilgrimage to our true selves, as Freeman calls it, is not in any way a form of narcissism or of selfish inner retreat – as at first sight it could well appear to be to some. In recognizing and appropriating our own birthright as children of God, we are then and only then fully ready to be the light to others which Christ called his disciples to be. I am reminded of a moving passage from the 1992 bestseller *A Return to Love*, by Marianne Williamson, in which she paraphrases *A Course in Miracles*:

Our deepest fear is not that we are inadequate.
Our deepest fear is that we are powerful beyond measure.
It is our light not our darkness, that most frightens us.
We ask ourselves, who am I to be brilliant,
gorgeous, talented and fabulous?
Actually, who are you NOT to be?
You are a child of God.
Your playing small doesn't serve the world,
There is nothing enlightened about shrinking
so that others won't feel insecure around you.
We were born to make manifest
the glory of God that is within us,
It's not just in some of us; it's in EVERYONE!
And as we let our own light shine,
we unconsciously give other people permission to do the same.
As we are liberated from our own fear,
our presence automatically liberates others![2]

As Freeman puts it, in meditation we are wholly inserted into the present – an experience of unity with our real self, with others, with the creation, and with its Creator. In this state of consciousness, we attain to the fullness of being.

THE BELFAST SEMINAR EXPERIENCE

I try to treat whoever I meet as an old friend.
This gives me a genuine feeling of happiness.
It is the practice of compassion.
H. H. the Dalai Lama

Looking closely at the heart and core of any major religion's spiritual practices reveals an amazing similarity. Meditation and contemplation, together with prayer in general, lead us to the deepest truths about ourselves, about the Ultimate Source of all being, and about our full relationship to the universe around us. The closer we come to the Great Center, the closer we draw to one another. This can't be said too often because initially, from a superficial examination, meditation can seem overly concerned with oneself or one's own religious commitment. This is perhaps particularly the case when, as with the WCCM approach, there is an almost universally practiced mantra and a heavy emphasis on a single religion – Christianity. Let me assure you that the literature, tapes, talks, and publications of WCCM, and especially the annual world seminars, make it clear that Dom Laurence Freeman and his far-flung community are fully open to other religions – and to the non-religious as well.

For example, the Belfast Seminar, held in October 2000, was the fourth and culminating event in a series begun in 1980, titled The Way of Peace. Significantly, as I've said, the chief figure involved in the dialogue with the community throughout this 20-year period was the world's best-known Buddhist leader, His Holiness the Dalai Lama. The earlier seminars had been held at the WCCM's London headquarters in 1980, when Freeman and the Dalai Lama met for the first time. They met next in 1994 in London for The Good Heart Seminar; in Bodhgaya, India, in 1998; and then in Florence, Italy, in 1999. My wife, Susan, and I went to Belfast, along with 500 other participants from various countries and belief systems. Belfast was chosen because it symbolizes perfectly the desperate need for peace and reconciliation in our modern world. (The total destruction of the World Trade Center in New York and of part of the Pentagon in the terrorist attack of September 11, 2001, has, of course, eclipsed most other symbols of mindless hatred and destruction since that time.)

The sessions were held in the spanking new convention center, the Belfast Waterfront Hall, in Belfast's historic harbor area, less than a mile (about one kilometer) from the spot where the ill-fated Titanic was built and launched by the famous shipbuilders Harland and Wolf.

The Dalai Lama (his ordinary name is Tendzin Gyatso) believes that informal conversations with other leaders are the best
way to get to a practical and honest understanding of complex
issues so that's how most of the dialogue was carried out. His
style is one of patience, formidable honesty, and humor. (As one
observer, an American psychologist from Massachusetts, put it,
"In the presence of His Holiness, no one can take himself or
herself too seriously.") But between all the talks and discussions
held in public, he managed to meet with hundreds of Belfast
youth, with survivors of the sectarian violence over the past 30
years, with business people, with hundreds in the streets in the
most troubled districts of that city, with local clergy – Roman
Catholic and Protestant – with city politicians, and also with
those in real power. For example, he had private talks with Mary
MacAleese, the President of the Republic of Ireland to the south.
She also gave a moving address to the assembly on ending the
cycle of violence in the name of Christ. Prime Minister Tony
Blair couldn't attend, but he sent a letter of commendation and
encouragement. He wrote: "The purpose of the Seminar could
not be more relevant to our goal of establishing lasting peace
and reconciliation in Northern Ireland."

*His Holiness the Dalai Lama and Father Laurence Freeman
in dialogue, Bodhgaya, India, December 1998.*

But perhaps the most important aspect of all was the Dalai Lama's insistence on the theme of becoming friends. The Buddha, once asked how important friendship was to the spiritual life, is reported to have said without hesitation that friendship was and *is* the spiritual life, the whole of it! The Dalai Lama himself was not calling for a masking of differences between religions, but simply asking that they become friends. Susan and I, and all those with whom we talked, experienced this reality for ourselves. Eating with members of other faiths, meditating with them for fairly lengthy periods of time, listening to their seemingly exotic music or chanting – all this and much more brought a surprising "high" which we will not soon forget.

Incidentally, in the late 1970s I once had a personal experience with the Dalai Lama that showed me all his talk about friendship was indeed matched by his own "walk." The first time I met him was in Heathrow Airport as I was arriving in London on business for *The Toronto Star*. I saw this saffron-robed, unmistakable figure, accompanied by two other monks, in a sort of small alcove, talking to two or three people. I got close up and when the opportunity came I introduced myself and asked for an interview. He was like a very friendly puppy in his greeting and willingness to give the time as soon as he was finished his informal meeting with the fans. Eventually, he answered my questions graciously, without the least projection of feeling hurried or hassled, and left me with the warm feeling that we were indeed friends. We have met several times since, once when I had the pleasure of introducing him to a packed Convocation Hall at the University of Toronto. He was always the same – open, compassionate, direct, and humbly a friend. If all religious leaders and all of their followers were to behave like this, we would have a very different kind of world.

That's what the WCCM is finally all about. Meditation is not just a tool, but an end in itself. It's about being a companion of God, a channel for the Divine Light. But its ultimate aim or goal is that of a world in which the Way of Peace is the new paradigm, not just for religions, but for the whole of humanity.

The closing interfaith service on Sunday, October 22, 2000, was held in the beautiful Church of Ireland (Anglican) Cathedral of St. Anne's, in downtown Belfast. The introit was done by Tibetan Buddhist monks from Gyudmed Tantric University, South India. There was Celtic music, by Irish artists – the Corrymeela Singers – as well as Irish dancing. There were Baha'i prayers for peace, and Hindu, Jewish, Muslim, Sikh, Christian, and Buddhist invocations and readings – a glorious plethora of the many-splendored ways in which the world's inhabitants render praise and thanksgivings to the one God. Roman Catholic representatives attended, as well as Protestants, including the Dean of the cathedral. It was a taste of what a harmonious future in Ulster could be.

Jesus once said to his disciples, "I have called you my friends."

Dom Laurence Freeman says, "What is the nature of friendship? It is reciprocated goodwill. We wish nothing but good towards the other for their own sake."

What other way to peace can there be?

Note: There is most likely a chapter of the WCCM near you. You can find out by contacting The John Main Institute, 7315 Brookville Road, Chevy Chase, MD, 208154, USA; or, in Canada, write to Meditatio Christian Meditation Community, PO Box 552, Station NDG, Montreal, Quebec, H4A 3P9. For the London, England, headquarters phone 0171-937-4679, or fax 0171-937-6790, or e-mail wccm@compuserve.com. Videos and tapes are available upon request.

VII

THE LABYRINTH PHENOMENON

The longest journey is the journey inwards of
him who has chosen his destiny.
Dag Hammarskjöld, *Markings*[1]

What I want to share here is a recently rediscovered, rapidly spreading spiritual practice which millions now enjoy. I'm talking about labyrinths, of course. The practice itself is called "walking the labyrinth." Susan and I have been experiencing it ourselves since about mid-1998. Its roots lie far off in the past, yet it's as contemporary as today's newspaper. It's free and it's open to anyone – for example, labyrinths are now being constructed in several American prisons and some hospitals, not to mention that hundreds of churches and even many gardens of private homes now have them too. What's more, the labyrinth's effectiveness can be self-tested and self-authenticated.

Before describing the labyrinth, however, let me digress briefly. When I was 19, I entered University College at The University of Toronto. I was enrolled in Honor Classics, a four-year, intensive course made up of reading in their original Greek and Latin most of the best-known writings of classical antiquity. This included Plato's *Republic* and other works; Aristotle's *Nichomachean Ethics*, and the *Ars Poetica*; the histories of Herodotus, Thucydides, Tacitus, Julius Caesar, Suetonius, and Pliny; the poetry of Homer, Pindar, Horace, Catullus, and many others; and the comedies and tragedies of the classical playwrights – from Aristophanes' *The Clouds* to the *Agamemnon* of Aeschylus.

At first, many of my friends and many of my elders were sceptical and even confused at this. They couldn't see the slightest possible use of studying "dead" languages and cultures in the 20th century. It would be less than useless in finding a job, they warned. One of my answers to them used to be, "I'm doing it because, not having the money myself, I can't afford to go to university any other way than by winning a scholarship." I really liked both Greek and Latin and had realized too that while winning a scholarship in those languages would be a difficult project there were nevertheless very few Grade 13 students in Ontario who could compete for them. The fact that I managed to win one (The Jarvis Scholarship, 1947) which not only paid entirely for the four years at the University of Toronto, but also for the many expensive books one had to purchase – all I had to do was keep getting first-class standing every year – was a major incentive. The course, with its two years of lectures in classical art and archaeology, and two in Oriental Literature, together with an introduction to the foundations of Western philosophy and ethics, grew more interesting every year.

I didn't find it a simple or easy road, but I became more and more certain I was in the right place. I won at least one additional scholarship each year, including the final year in which I was awarded the McCaul Gold Medal for highest standing in Classics at the University of Toronto for the year and, almost simultaneously, a Rhodes Scholarship for three years at Oriel College, Oxford. Again, I chose Classics (called Literae Humaniores or Greats) and found that they ploughed that field both "narrow and very deep," as a Canadian fellow-classicist had warned me before I went over.

There's a significant point to what perhaps might otherwise seem a proud, self-serving account. I don't claim much credit for any of it. Prayer was "answered" in an astonishing way. Just as I was preparing to write this chapter, though, an image from long ago flashed to my mind. In it, I was sitting in a small lecture room just off the second or third floor at the Royal Ontario Museum, Toronto, with a half-dozen other students, while the professor droned on about the contrast between Ionic and Doric-style columns, especially when you compared both with the later, Corinthian mode. He was showing slides; the room was darkened. Sleep hovered nearby. Suddenly, I was awakened out of a semi-torpor as I heard him begin speaking about the Palace at Cnossos, in Crete, and about a 4,000-year-old labyrinth there, probably the oldest in the Western world. I sat bolt upright and looked at the slide on the screen. The image was extraordinarily intriguing, speaking somehow to my depths, and what the professor was saying about it was even more so. Little did I dream then that about 40 years later I would be writing in a very large newspaper, *The Toronto Star*, the biggest in Canada, and then much more fully in this book, about this same labyrinth and, even more to the point, about its successors today and their relevance for the spiritual awakening which is now going on everywhere.

This, of course, is not the place for a description of the Minoan civilization which had its center at the Palace at Cnossos and which bloomed in Crete, and throughout the Mediterranean world from about 2800 BCE and then (roughly in 1450 BCE) suddenly disappeared from the face of the Earth. This cataclysm was possibly due to vast tidal waves and upheavals caused by the same earthquake that seared, twisted, and scorched the nearby island of Santorini. Some scholars believe that the two islands of Atlantis, cited by Plato in *The Timaeus*, may have disappeared at the same time for the same reasons.

What's important here is the Cnossos labyrinth, a coiled, seven-circuit, intricate series of infolding paths, with one way in (and one way out), to and from the very center. This labyrinth was celebrated on ancient coins minted close by and in Greek mythology (remember the Minotaur, the monster who dwelled there, and his vanquisher, the Greek hero, Theseus). But most important, it seems to be a kind of archetype or expression of something deeply held in the human unconscious. Some experts speak of it as a kind of "divine imprint" in the human psyche. Its name comes from the ancient double-headed axe, the *labris*, which is evident in its design. Whenever I see one in a sketch or view a real labyrinth from above, I'm reminded of the two lobes of the brain. The winding but tightly woven "knit" of the pathways reminds me of the brain also, in simplified form. That the design comes from some innate place within us is also strongly suggested by the fact that the labyrinth – as distinct from a maze which has many dead-ends and whose object seems to be to utterly confuse anyone caught in it – shows up as a sacred place of pilgrimage and self-discovery in many different cultures and places around the world.

Many, if not most, of the great cathedrals of Europe have labyrinths etched or otherwise marked – say by certain patterns and pavings of bricks or stones – into the floors, often just in front of the chancel area, as at Chartres Cathedral in France, just south of Paris, (of which more in a moment). There were labyrinths, for example, in the cathedrals of Sens, Arras,

Amiens, Reims, and Auxerre; and in smaller forms, as at Lucca Cathedral, in Italy, just Northwest of Florence, where there are "finger labyrinths" on the walls of the cathedral itself, which can be traced as a kind of symbolic "walking" instead. But the

Chartres labyrinth pattern

circular, spiralling pattern has been found not just in churches, but almost everywhere: in prehistoric caves, carved into rocks, woven into the design of baskets or blankets, reproduced on coins and jewelry in such places as Scandinavia, Peru, Syria, Egypt, and Arizona. The Hopi Indians of the American Southwest have found it a useful spiritual tool. It is still used by devout Buddhists and Hindus today. For those interested in the history and the locations of other Christian abbeys, churches, and cathedrals in Europe with labyrinth connections, I strongly recommend Jean Villette's 1995 book, *The Enigma of the Labyrinth*.

Villette describes how in some places later church authorities tried to erase all traces of their labyrinths for a range of reasons, including iconoclasm – motivated perhaps by fears of paganism or the like – and because some viewed them as an interruption to the services, with people sometimes parading around irreverently in the middle of the liturgy. In the case of Reims Cathedral, for example, one canon, who was troubled by the noise caused by children and the idle walking the labyrinth while worship was going on, made an offer of a thousand pounds for its removal! According to Villette, the period of the 1700s saw devastating attacks on many of "the most lovely monuments" of the early Gothic era.

But when we say that labyrinths were "used," what does that mean? Used how and for what? People new to this whole concept have a right and need to ask this specific question. While one of the labyrinth's greatest appeals is that you don't have to be a believer of any recognized kind to use it successfully, its shape and almost universal association with religion/spirituality and the sacred indicate that it has something to do with a pilgrimage or journey to the center – perhaps to the center of oneself, perhaps to God the center of all things, perhaps to the core of one's past, even, perhaps, a journey back to the womb and beyond. The basic idea seems to have been the universal concept of going to a goal at the end of a laborious journey (the hero's quest of mythology and legends). It symbolized for some the passage between birth and death. For Christians, it was the pilgrim's search for the Holy City (i.e., Heaven or the full Presence of the Divine itself).

It is significant, for example, that in past centuries, especially after about 900 CE, European Christians who could afford it felt it to be a once-in-a-lifetime obligation to make a holy pilgrimage to Jerusalem. However, the Crusades (the first was in 1096–1099; the eighth and last was in 1270 CE) created such uncertainties and hostilities along the route that these journeys came to be looked upon as totally unsafe. Instead, the cathedrals being built in and after this period incorporated labyrinths as an alternative form of pilgrimage, a symbolic "journey to Jerusalem." The circular path was called "The Way to Jerusalem," while the center spot of quiet reflection or meditation was called "The New Jerusalem."

What is truly interesting, though, is the manner in which this ancient, mystical device has, with no mumbo jumbo or New Age "buzz" being responsible, suddenly burst from or upon the consciousness of modern men and women. There are now well over 1,000 labyrinths in the U.S. alone. In the beautiful region of southern Ontario where Susan and I live, there are several, mostly on "power centers" or spots in the Beaver Valley traditionally associated with healing energies by the First Nations peoples. But there are hundreds of them right across Canada today, including about 65 in Ontario, mostly in the Greater Toronto Area. One of the most dramatic in this country, however, is the 11-circuit labyrinth (some early labyrinths, such as the one at Cnossos, were seven circuits) in the heart of Toronto's downtown business district. It is situated outdoors near a fountain and is always open. You can observe sales staff from the adjacent shopping mall, The Eaton Centre, or Bay Street brokers, and/or street people – in other words, people of every background – walking there at almost any hour of the day. We don't get down to the city very often (it's about a three-hour drive) but whenever we do one or both of us make(s) the time to spend the 20 to 25 minutes required to go slowly to the center of the labyrinth, pause a few moments for centering or simple silence, and then to wind slowly back to the entrance again.

> *The labyrinth is an archetype of wholeness*
> *that helps us rediscover the depths of our souls.*
> *We are not human beings on a spiritual path*
> *but spiritual beings on a human path.*
> Canon Lauren Artress, *Walking a Sacred Path*[2]

Christians in particular seem to be leading the way in the labyrinth movement. One of the leading figures in labyrinth "revival," the Reverend Canon Dr. Lauren Artress, an associate minister at the Grace Episcopal Cathedral, San Francisco, and author of *Walking a Sacred Path*, is the founder of Veriditas: The Worldwide Labyrinth Project. Her mission is to help those interested in reinstating the labyrinth as a spiritual tool worldwide. She visited the well-known (for its gorgeous stained glass windows and now for its centuries-old labyrinth) Cathedral of Notre Dame de Chartres, usually simply called Chartres, in the early 1990s and came back thrilled with the experience of walking its labyrinth.

The labyrinth at Chartres – an 11-circuit model – was first built in 1201. In 1992, almost 800 years later, Artress decided to build one like it on top of the famous Nob Hill overlooking the Pacific Ocean where Grace Cathedral, San Francisco, stands. It now has become the most famous labyrinth in the entire Western world. By 1999, over one million people had walked its paths and found its secrets to be balm for the soul. There is a labyrinth (constructed as many are today on a very large canvas base) inside the cathedral as well, but the truly amazing thing is the way in which the idea has caught on. People come to Grace Cathedral and then go home to form groups to "turn it into flesh" at their own church, village open space, or a myriad of other appropriate places. Artress writes: "The labyrinth is an archetype of wholeness that helps us rediscover the depths of our souls." On the Veriditas website, there is a piece done by Peter Corbett that says, "One of the symptoms of spiritual crisis is a lack of centeredness, a lack of awareness of the spiritual nature of our true selves. Until our spiritual center is restored we will continue to drift as individuals and as a society."

You have to walk the labyrinth yourself – not once or twice, but several times – to know what it can do or mean for you and your life. The great thing about it is that it brings insight, a relaxation from stress, an uncanny sense of making a new beginning, of "peeling off" one's old skin, like a snake being renewed, or, better, like the metamorphosis of a caterpillar into a butterfly. Sometimes one's meditative winding in and out of the sudden twists and spiralling turns brings the sense of retracing one's life, the good and the bad alike. Then, the turning back and unwinding softly down brings a strange sensibility of inner peace and focus. People experience a wide variety of feelings and thoughts at the center, from pure stillness to a new vision of meaning and purpose. Having walked one many times now over the past four years, I can personally testify that no two labyrinth experiences have been identically the same. The potential for fresh self-knowledge or a different perspective on one's relationships to others, oneself, and the universe seems almost endless.

Everyone I have met who has encountered the labyrinth phenomenon for themselves communicates the very strong awareness or sense that their "finding" it was not sheer accident. I don't mean to get entrapped in a kind of sentimental, "mushy" kind of thinking here. I'm inclined to be sceptical about people's claims to have had "God's guidance" in every phase of their lives and at every turn. But I do believe that the Divine Wisdom is with us all, to be discovered certainly at critical moments where not mere incidentals but the key decisions of our lives are being made. In any event, let me just say honestly that the way Susan and I "discovered" the labyrinth had so many synchronicities about it that it seemed "meant to be."

The labyrinth is a path of prayer for all people seeking the Divine, regardless of the tradition in which we stand. The winding path leading to the center serves as a mirror to reflect the movement of the Spirit in our lives.

From a sign at the entrance to the labyrinth in Orlando, Florida, at Woodlawn Memorial Park and Funeral Home.

In early 1999, we went to the Gulf Coast of Florida for a seven-week holiday, rest, and a time of exploration with a view to future newspaper articles. It was the longest time we had ever spent away from home and duties, and we naturally enjoyed it to the full. However, after about four weeks at a beachfront motel near Destin, on the "Panhandle," we began to feel an urge to move on. Since I had never even once visited Disney World, Susan decided to include Orlando on our route. So, having visited friends in Tampa for a couple of days and having spent some time exploring the historic old town of St. Augustine's, we marked Orlando on the map and headed there.

We never did get to Disney World. As Susan drove and I read the relevant information, including a file I'd brought with me stuffed with information about the area, I came across some notes I had made a year or so earlier about the labyrinth. I grew quite excited as I read how there was a principal example of one in or around Orlando, and a unique one, designed with circling rows of conch shells, at Ormond Beach as well. After a certain amount of searching and running around in general, we learned that the Orlando sacred walk was situated on the grounds of a vast parkland-like funeral and cemetery center, Woodlawn Memorial Park. This may sound a little macabre, but I assure you that the opposite was the case.

First, the 11-circuit labyrinth lies far away from the head office and there are no burial markers anywhere to be seen. In fact, it lies in the midst of a wonderful orange orchard, with warbling birds – some of which I'd never seen before – and extensive lawns all about. In front of it towers the largest free-standing mosaic mural of the life of Christ I have ever seen in all my travels. It has 23 scenes from the life of Jesus, painted by two famous Hollywood sister artists, Venetian Epler and Dauphine Huntington, and made by two Italian mosaicists in a process involving roughly 11 million tiny pieces of Venetian stained glass. But our attention, as we stood at the entrance to the mosaic early one breathtakingly beautiful morning, was not really on the mosaic. We were eager to make our very first walk on this strange, new-to-us "pilgrimage tool." I should add here that a sign at the starting point noted that the average time to go from the outside to the center and then, after a pause, back again, was about 20 minutes. (An exact replica of the one paved in Bercheres stone [a light-colored sandstone] before the chancel at Chartres Cathedral, the labyrinth is approximately 42 feet (13 meters) in diameter. The total distance in and out is about one-third of a mile (0.65 kilometers).

There were no other people anywhere around. All was still, save for the chirping and singing of the birds. We took our time, slowed down inwardly, and just tried in a relaxed manner to "let go." Bob Neel, head of the Woodlawn Chartres Labyrinth Society and the main inspiration behind the whole project there, admits there are as many ways of using the labyrinth as there are different types and personalities. But, in his literature, available at the entrance, he suggests five ways that he has found useful himself. Since he has walked this kind of path now in hundreds of places, including at Chartres itself and at the conch construction at Ormond, he certainly merits a hearing.

The path of image

Neel says that once the mind is quiet (some advance deep breathing is recommended before entering), the walker may experience memories or dream fragments floating to awareness. Allow them to expand within your imagination. Active imagination techniques are very useful on the labyrinth. Talk to the characters in any dream or story line that arises. (We met none ourselves.)

The path of silence

Quiet the mind on the walk in and then enter into a deep sense of silence in the center of the labyrinth. Neel quotes Thomas Carlyle (1795–1881) with this line: "*Silence* is the element in which great things fashion themselves together." We have cited the truth of this aphorism elsewhere regarding meditation and prayer.

A path of prayer

In its simplest form, the walk is indeed a path of prayer. Seekers can go in, allow their minds to quieten, and then begin to pray for whatever is needed in their lives. He notes, it may be a prayer for courage, release from fears, guidance, or perseverance.

A place of release and renewal

Here you'll find you can release old resentments, losses, fears, and hearts hardened due to past hurts. Walkers can release the feelings as they arise and then ask for guidance, forgiveness, or whatever may be needed for healing.

Asking a question

A question of discernment can be asked at the outset of the labyrinth walk. If you are in the midst of making a decision about a move, a new job, or a relationship, Neel suggests you can "try it on" in the labyrinth. Our thinking, judgmental, or fearful mind becomes transparent in the labyrinth, he has found. We see through that which holds us back; we can discern more accurately what we truly need to live our lives in service to God and others.

Susan and I decided just to "hang loose" and see what came up. Slowly walking along, loop after loop, sometimes sweeping close to the very center and then suddenly taking a turn to the outer edge, the stillness outside and the deepening, responsive stillness within, gradually brought about what I can only describe as a change of consciousness. What Blake called "The Doors of Perception" seemed indeed to be changing, opening up, making us more and more awake or aware. For me, it seemed as though I was "walking" through my life to that date – noting in particular those moments or weeks of trauma of some sort or another, as well as those key events where my goals and purposes took the most fruitful directions. It was uncanny in one way, but I felt peaceful as a process of transformation seemed to be going on deep within.

At the center, there were no "voices," visions, or instant illuminations – just a feeling of being "home" and of wanting to utter a silent prayer of thanks at the absolute goodness of the Creator throughout our lives. Winding, or rather unwinding, back again seemed the right time for decisions about inner changes, about what the Anglican and Episcopal Prayer Books mean when they talk about "walking in newness of life." It felt like a chance to begin again, as though the past had been purged and exciting opportunities lay ahead.

We were both so impressed by our first labyrinth walk that we returned the two following mornings to repeat the practice. Then, having heard of the conch shell design labyrinth at Ormond Beach, we drove north and east to find it. Arriving there late one hot afternoon, we searched for more than an hour and were thinking of giving up when Susan spotted a woman setting up a fancy tea party in a garden just behind the closed Information Center. (It was a special Valentine's Day gift for a recently married couple.) Sue asked the woman whether she had ever heard of a labyrinth made of conch shells around Ormond Beach. To Sue's complete surprise, the woman replied instantly, "Yes, ma'am. My sister created it herself." She then proceeded to give us simple, clear directions for how to get there. She said it was on the northern edge of town, on the corner of U.S. Highway 1, just behind a Legacy Golf Store. That sounded just a little tacky, we thought, but when we finally got there, the location and the labyrinth were scenic and very quiet. It was laid out on a little knoll. There was a large trout-pond beside it, the sea lapped the sands close by, and the novel concept of using conch shells for the seven-circuit labyrinth itself – with occasional large rocks as markers, and a tree at the very core, symbolizing Jerusalem – all added to the charm. There was no sign with instructions, no money to be paid, no list of rules, and no denominational or faith symbols whatever. It lies open to all. The sea's murmuring lent a primordial, even cosmic dimension to the walk, as all stresses and tensions slipped away. We have walked scores of labyrinths since, but none has surpassed that one in the inspiration and peace it offered. There was utter simplicity at its highest.

It's interesting that Robert Neel's first experience with labyrinths was walking the conch labyrinth with his daughter. He was so impressed and so persuaded that the idea or "tool" had a latent, transformative power, that he determined to build the one at Woodlawn already described. Immediately after the Ormond walk, Neel said he was very puzzled: "How could walking a meandering path make me feel so deeply centered?" he asked himself. But it did, and he was moved to action. He took the time first, however, to travel to Europe to see the labyrinth at Chartres, the finger labyrinths at Lucca and elsewhere, and, of course, the two (now three, with two outdoors) at Grace Cathedral, San Francisco. Together with Artress and other teams elsewhere, especially at the St. Louis Labyrinth Society, Missouri, Neel has become one of the key figures in labyrinth promotion in the West. Apart from his own Woodlawn publications, he has been widely featured in the increasing media coverage being given to this topic. *The Toronto Star* has published not just my column about the labyrinth but several major articles. In 1998–1999 alone, a number of top media outlets, including a *New York Times* front-page cover story, segments on ABC/TV *Evening News* with Peter Jennings, and on MTV, together with numerous magazine features, brought the phenomenon of walking the labyrinth into fuller public consciousness. There have since then been features in *Ladies Home Journal* and on the spiritual segment of *Oprah*, as well.

In an article he wrote for the official publication of the U.S.-based International Cemetery and Funeral Association, July 1999 issue, Neel wrote the following:

> *Why does the labyrinth attract people? It is a tool to guide healing, deepen self-knowledge and empower creativity. Walking the labyrinth clears the mind and gives insight to their spiritual journey. It urges action. It calms people in the throes of life transitions. It helps one find the inner self. It is a place to walk and meditate, solve problems and talk and pray to your God.*

Some call walking this particular path a "walking meditation," others use the term "prayer in motion," and yet others again speak about an "invitation to the sacred, a journey of discovery about oneself and about one's relationship to the Divine."

According to Sylvia Senesky, a Jungian psychoanalyst who now conducts workshops and seminars throughout the province of Ontario, on labyrinths and on creating sacred spaces generally, there's no right way to walk a labyrinth:

> *Perhaps you have a problem to solve; you may repeat a Hindu mantra or a Christian prayer. You can walk alone or in a group, you can chant, cry, or dance. You do need to walk*

it with the right intention. You need to walk it consciously;
you need to be open, and you need to prepare yourself be-
cause you're walking in a sacred place.

Senesky, as reported in *The Toronto Star* (October 31, 1998) by
journalist Kathryn Korchuk, first encountered the labyrinth while
studying with the American psychologist and author, Jean Houston, who had visited Chartres Cathedral. That was in 1987. Dr.
Lauren Artress, of Grace Cathedral, a psychotherapist as well as
an Episcopal priest, studied with Houston – by a synchronicity
– in 1991. That same year she made the first of Grace Cathedral's
labyrinth walks.

A TOOL FOR TRANSFORMATION

The Labyrinth seems to tap into a forgotten,
archetypal reservoir that connects us with the universe,
our ancient predecessors, and ourselves.
Robert Ferre, *The Labyrinth Revival?*[3]

There is so much more to the labyrinth than I have described
here – for example, the whole matter of its connections to ancient astrology. Was the original seven-circuit labyrinth of Cnossos
a reflection of the path of the planet Mercury through one of its
solar years, as viewed from Earth, as Robert Ferre of the St.
Louis Labyrinth Project suggests in his excellent 1996 book, *The
Labyrinth Revival*? At Chartres, some researchers believe that
there are 112 "lunations" in the design (along the circumfer-
ence) which were used to calculate the date of Easter. Easter is,
of course, always the first Sunday after the first full moon following the spring equinox near March 21 (in the northern hemi-
sphere). Others today are researching the psychological and even

the physiological aspects of this very ancient symbol: for example, not only does it have a strong resemblance to the shape of the human brain, but also to the way our "guts" fit into the space above the pelvic bones. Like the "labyrinth" within the human ear, the so-called "middle ear," it is a balancing device, but it's for the mind and spirit instead. Like anything else that has enormous potential and operates in mystical or hidden ways, it can be exploited by the unscrupulous who see an opportunity for financial gain. Those kinds of people are always with us. Some enthusiasts get carried away in making extravagant claims, as if it were a form of magic or a "get-well" machine. It's not. With that caveat, however, I don't just believe, I know, that its rediscovery at this momentous time, a time of great peril and of unprecedented opportunity for our race, is not accidental. It is being offered by the cosmos, by the Divine Mind or God, as a key tool for the rediscovery of ourselves and the necessary empowerment for the way ahead. I agree with Ferre when he says that in its very simplicity lies its strength. He notes that it doesn't challenge the mind, it relaxes it. There is no need for any struggle. It takes us on a journey which predates history. It "unites us with an ancient and forgotten part of ourselves."[4] Ferre sounds like Kabat-Zinn and other meditation experts when he describes the experience as taking us away from "doing" and into "being." Personally, I like very much the way in which the labyrinth can be used by people who, for whatever reason, have no place for religion in their lives; I like the fact that Hindus and those in that tradition can see ways of using it to "tune their chakras" or body energy centers, and that members of all other faiths can enter "the cosmic dance" at this point. But I'm particularly moved by its direct relevance for those on a spiritual path seeking to know the Divine and to be transformed.

"It's a crucible for change," says Canon Lauren Artress, "a field of light." I know from experience that in that crucible and light, stress melts away or is transcended.

PART THREE

SOURCES AND MANTRAS

VIII

FROM THE OLD TESTAMENT
OR HEBREW BIBLE

When I look at the contemporary scene,
I have a mixture of feelings.
In large part, I am saddened because much of
what I see are watered-down versions of
original teachings that have been made
palatable to Western consumers.
George Feuerstein,
for 25 years an interpreter, to the West, of Eastern traditions[1]

INTRODUCTION

Anyone making a spiritual response to stress has a time-tested, rich, and highly rewarding treasury of wisdom and inspiration from which to draw. As we shall see in a moment, and as I personally believe most deeply, this treasury has been greatly expanded and enriched by our increasing familiarity today with the practices and written resources of other major world religions. Nevertheless, it is with the Jewish and Christian material that the majority of people in the Western world are still most at home. It has a ring of our own past about it, a comforting "feel," even though there may well be comparatively few churchgoers now who really know its power from their own experience. Even today there's a Bible in almost every home. But it usually gathers dust as it lies unopened.

What follows immediately, and in the next two chapters as well, is a setting out of specific passages from various sources that have been tried and experimented with by millions through the centuries. Importantly for our immediate purposes, they have been put to tough, practical use in my life also. I must be bold and wholly candid in underlining this fact. This is not a facile repetition of pious phrases for some special effect. It's an honest attempt to share only what I know myself has worked for me and for countless numbers of friends, parishioners, students, readers, viewers, and acquaintances throughout a lifetime. Without such resources, what Jon Kabat-Zinn has dubbed "the full catastrophe" (the stresses and strains of a very active life) might well have overwhelmed me long ago.

THE OLD TESTAMENT OR HEBREW BIBLE

Jews were not to think of God as a Big Brother
watching their every move from above; instead,
they were to cultivate a sense of God within each human being
so that our dealings with others became sacred encounters.

Karen Armstrong, *History of God*[2]

This collection of 39 unique books of varying lengths, by a wide range of authors over several centuries, and including everything from moral truths to erotic poetry, is an inexhaustible fount of inspiration, illumination, and encouragement. Many millions down the ages and all over the world at this moment find it to be an irreplaceable resource for a creative approach to stress in their lives. I could not begin to list or mention all that it contains bearing on our particular theme. What follows is but a sampling of key parts that I know from experience can work for anyone regardless of their own faith – or lack of one that is recognized by some organized body. They have been an enormous blessing, through both good times and bad times, for me and for those I have known best.

GENESIS

The story of the Creation of all there is, from distant galaxies to the human race, is not an attempt to give a scientific or historical description. It's not about a scientific anthropology, biology, or any of the other "ologies" contained in modern textbooks. It operates at a much deeper level. It contains the inner, religious and spiritual truth that alone gives a soul-satisfying meaning and purpose to life itself.

It cannot be overstated that the opening verses of Genesis – as we have already partly seen – resound with themes that are the very foundation of Jewish, Christian, and Muslim spirituality, echoed also in most other major religions. That we come from God, that we are in God's image, and especially that we live, move, and breathe by the "breath" of God, means that the ultimate source of the entire universe, including other possible universes, is *on our side*, is actually both *around* us and *within* us. There can be no fuller assurance, no medication or drug, no substance, no technique that can work the wonders that just knowing this truth and constantly living in it and affirming it can afford. Every conscious breath we take, moment by moment for the rest of our lives, can powerfully remind us of this reality.

This, as we have seen already, is by no means to disparage the proper place and role for specific medicines, other treatments, and focused training in stress "management." Contrary to the attitudes and arguments of some would-be "stress experts," antidepressants, tranquilizers, and a host of other therapeutic tools are not something we should feel guilty about using (when properly administered by doctors). They can be at times as much a gift of God's goodness and love as prayer or scriptures. The great difference between medications or other techniques and a fully spiritual response, however, is that the former deal mainly with symptoms while the latter goes to the root of the problem.

The Genesis stories of Abraham, Isaac, Jacob, and the others, are filled with lessons and nurture for the soul. I don't wish to repeat here what I have written about them elsewhere, but they are well-worth re-reading by anyone concerned about or being overwhelmed by stress. Notice in particular how God seems to be more fully revealed and known precisely at the moments of greatest crisis: for example, at Bethel, where a very frightened, weary, and lonely Jacob, with his life apparently in an impossible mess, dreams his famous dream of the ladder to heaven, with the angels of God ascending and descending upon it. In the morning he cries out in thanksgiving and jubilation. The dream's meaning has become clear and he expresses this in some of the most encouraging words ever uttered: "Surely God was in this place, and I knew it not" (Genesis 28:16).

I have found it helpful as well, when in an uncritical, devotional mode, to read these sagas and listen to the subtle nuances of the conversations and other direct dealings with the mystery of God. There is a strength to the narrative, an immediacy and an intimacy, that encourages one to be more bold in one's own inner conversations with the Divine. Also, it is empowering to hear how very human these patriarchs were. For example, Jacob, the deceiver (yet the one called to be Israel and the begetter of the 12 heads of the tribes of Israel), knew anxiety and depression as well as any person today.

EXODUS

Moses, of course, is the most exalted of leaders in the founding and history of the Jewish people. His is a towering presence; so much so, in fact, that many centuries later, the writers of the Christian gospels would conceptualize and set forth Jesus, called Christ or the anointed of God, in terms of a "prophet like unto Moses." The infant Jesus is threatened by Herod just as Moses was by a pharaoh. Jesus comes up out of Egypt just as Moses comes from Egypt to the verge of the Promised Land. The Sermon on the Mount of Matthew's gospel is meant to be seen as a second giving of the Law in its new form just as Moses received the Ten Commandments and brought them down from Mount Sinai.

But again, we are shown the hero's total humanity. Before God called him to lead his people out of Egypt, Moses was a murderer who had "snapped" in the presence of an injustice – the sight of an Egyptian striking an Israelite (Exodus 2:11–12). You would have thought that the opportunity to be a kind of messianic figure delivering his kindred out of bondage would have come to Moses as a great honor and grace. But the text makes it plain that, even though he was given the revelatory vision of the burning bush and had an amazing encounter with Yahweh, Moses hung back and fired off excuses when challenged to accept the task of liberator.

He whined and whinged because of flooding feelings of inadequacy and overall angst. No doubt his bowels were churning and his blood pressure was at an all-time high. He may even have had a sudden panic attack. His answer to "the Lord" was instantaneous: "Who am I, that I should go unto Pharaoh, and that I should bring forth the children of Israel out of Egypt?" (Exodus 3:11). God expressly promises to be with Moses and that his leadership will be a great success. Nevertheless, Moses remains full of terrified doubts. God shows him miracles – his staff becomes a serpent and then a staff again; his hand becomes leprous and is healed; he is told to pour river water on dry land and watch as it turns to blood – yet he makes another whimper: "O my Lord, I have never been eloquent, neither in the past nor even now that you have spoken to your servant; but I am slow of speech, and of a slow tongue" (Exodus 4:10).

Moses pleads for God to send somebody else. Understandably (purely in human terms and as modern critics would say, anthropomorphically), God becomes angry and tells Moses that his brother Aaron is eloquent and will act as spokesman for his words. Only then does Moses relent and accept the responsibility.

Even so, he remains a difficult, volatile candidate for the leadership he so reluctantly accepts. At almost the very moment that fresh anxieties and stresses arise, Moses gets worked up over Jewish criticisms of his decisions and files an urgent complaint: "Then Moses turned again to the Lord and said, 'O Lord, why have you mistreated this people? Why did you ever send me? Since I first came to Pharaoh to speak in your name, he has mistreated this people, and you have done nothing at all to deliver your people'" (Exodus 5:22–23).

You can see this kind of dialogue throughout Moses' life. But, in fact, it is an aspect of the response to stress that characterizes the lives of most of those who have remained highly committed to divine living and service from the beginning of recorded history. The greatest witness to this very human side of our ongoing dialogue with God is the Book of Psalms.

The truth is that in my own life, like millions of others, I have found these stories and many others like them in the Old Testament to be a great aid in alleviating stress. It is human to recoil sometimes, even if only momentarily, from a sudden challenge to take on a role or a responsibility one has never tackled before. I most certainly felt that way the first time I faced an open microphone at a radio station and opened the phone lines to take on all comers in a program called *Harpur's Heaven and Hell*. Part of me wished I was anywhere else but in that studio. However, just knowing that this nervousness is perfectly natural and human takes the "awfulness" out of it. We see it in a much less terrifying light. The Divine Mystery "knows our every weakness" and is familiar with all our insecurities. Knowing this and knowing that with every divine imperative or invitation God promises to be with us, can relieve inner tensions that will yield to nothing else.

The rest of the Book of Exodus is "a good read" (and for many people a good deal more as well) and contains, among other things, the giving of the Law of Moses or the Ten Commandments (Exodus 20:1–17). But for our immediate concern it can be passed over.

JOSHUA

For Jewish, Christian, and other believers or would-be believers, the Book of Joshua (which, like "Jesus," means deliverer or savior) is of deep significance. Scholars today believe it was written, at least in its earliest form, in about 1000 BCE. From our point of view some 3,000 years later, the book's description of the conquest of Canaan is quite off-putting. It comes complete with slaughters of innocents, attempts at genocide, and a picture of God that at times is quite shocking from any perspective, be it moral or theological. For example, the popular American folk song which describes how "Joshua fit the battle of Jericho and the walls came a-tumbling down" says nothing about the fact that Joshua and his troops rushed in over the rubble of the walls and "devoted to destruction by the edge of the sword all in the city, both men and women, young and old, oxen, sheep, and donkeys." Next they torched and "*burned down the city, and everything in it*" (Joshua 6:20–24). We are reminded of the slaughter of Taliban prisoners by Northern Alliance troops in Afghanistan in November 2001.

This kind of scorched-earth, blitzkrieg approach is used in varying degrees by the invading Israelites throughout the entire conquest. That was a very long time ago, however, and must be comprehended in the light of changing understandings of who and what God is. (See Karen Armstrong's bestseller, *A History of God*.) Atrocities committed by Christians millennia later during the Crusades, at the Reformation, or later in the conquest of the

Americas, also have to be examined to give a wider perspective. This whole subject belongs to an important debate, but I leave that to others for now.

What's important here is what the book contains by way of insights and/or resources for responding to stress in the turmoil and pressures of modern living. There are strong, solid reasons for keeping Joshua in mind when troubles and sometimes even joys leave our nerves quivering and our nights without sleep.

The commissioning of Joshua

The first chapter of the Book of Joshua contains some of the most encouraging, bracing, "stress-busting" words ever written. They are much more powerful than any pill or exotic technique. I have always turned to them, ever since I was a young man just entering university for the first time, many years ago. I know personally many hundreds of people who make them their constant daily companion. They can be treated just like any other mantra. Find a quiet place inside or out – or while walking alone – and slowly repeat the verses. Pay attention to your breathing, making it drawn-out, deep, and in and out from your nose only, if possible. Do this in a relaxed manner if you can, and for at least 15 minutes. Try it especially on first waking, in whatever moments of opportunity present themselves during your day, and particularly just before nodding off to sleep at night.

These are the words: "Be strong and courageous; do not be frightened or dismayed, for the Lord your God is with you wherever you go" (Joshua1:9, see also verses 6 and 7).

Significantly, Joshua himself never forgot this command not to be afraid. Those familiar with the balance of the book know that he repeated these words to the children of Israel at times of crisis, and that God's ongoing dialogue with him resounded again and again with "Be not afraid…for I am with you." Readers of my newspaper and other work know that the most characteristic words of Jesus – the later Joshua or Yeshua – were precisely these: "Fear not, for..."

LIVING LIFE IN YOUR OWN "ARMOR"

Most people, believers or not, know of the famous story of David and Goliath. However, they may never have read it for themselves, or, if they have, they may not be able to call to mind much of the story itself.

I remember once, at a university party of some kind, getting into a discussion with two classical professors. They were arguing the relative merits of Michelangelo's famous sculpture of David, poised in the calm moment before slinging his stone and killing the huge Philistine champion; and Bernini's statue of David, showing the tense action as the youth actually winds up to throw. They were erudite and eloquent. Michelangelo's version, they pointed out, was typically classical. The ideal man in the moment of quiet, almost philosophical calm before the fight. Bernini's was more typically Hellenistic – what is central is the depiction of the human form in the contortions and emotional throes of genuine, heroic activity. But they knew nothing, it seemed, of the surrounding text in the only source, 1 Samuel 17: 31ff, or of the spiritual wallop it carries.

Some of this message is so obvious – for example, the deep symbolism of the stripling youth (the average human soul) facing the fearsome, towering warrior (the rigors and stresses of "the full catastrophe"), and winning out through a combination of courage, skill, and a profound assurance of being in and with the strength of God.

What can be easily missed, however, are the details of the saga just before the encounter, which both these Renaissance artists portray in marble. When David comes before King Saul and offers to do mortal combat with Goliath, Saul is sceptical and points out David's youth and inexperience compared with the giant's professional fighting reputation and sheer size. David then makes a resounding declaration of his own successes and particularly of his firm faith that God is with him.

Saul reluctantly accepts him as Israel's contender, but, just to reassure himself, he gets the young would-be warrior to put on his (Saul's) armor. 1 Samuel 17:38–39 reads as follows:

> *Saul clothed David with his armor; he put a bronze helmet on his head and clothed him with a coat of mail. David strapped Saul's sword over the armor, and he tried in vain to walk, for he was not used to them. Then David said to Saul, "I cannot walk with these; for I am not used to them." So David removed them.*

The spiritual meaning for us as we seek a successful working response to stress in our lives is potent. The moral is that we must always do battle with our own "armor" on. In other words, we must resist the ever-present and subtle temptation to be somebody else instead of our real, authentic selves. When the stress and strain of living become too much, and disaster (real or imagined) looms, it is enticing to wish or think we should be somebody else, or very much like them. Instead of realizing the power that lies within us and without, instead of trusting in the personal gifts God has given to each one of us to help us overcome hurdles, find peace within, and keep on keeping on, we make guilt-traps for ourselves; we wish we could be like some acquaintance, or even like someone we have never met but deeply admire.

"My own weapons, my own armor, my own resources empowered by the Spirit" – that's the sort of unspoken slogan or mantra under which the person-becoming-wholly-whole can successfully do battle. Of course, one still enlists the help and assistance of doctors, psychiatrists, clergy, or counselors of appropriate kinds, if and as they may be required. But the point is to avoid being tricked into ever imagining that somebody else's path ought or must be the one for you.

DEPRESSION AND THOUGHTS OF SUICIDE HAUNT THE GREAT PROPHET ELIJAH

And after the fire a sound of sheer silence.

1 Kings 19:12

Unfortunately, it is widely thought that to profess to be a believer – whether Jewish, Christian, Muslim, or Hindu – means to lay claim to a kind of perfection or saintliness beyond the reach of others. The same is true regarding those persons, past or present, said to be holy or saintly. This, of course, is a blatant falsehood – one that has a lot of sting in its tail, however. Brought up in a very conservative, evangelical background myself, I can testify to the negative power of such a concept. It produced much unnecessary stress and was a dragon I slew only by a further, deeper reading of sacred texts as I reached early teens.

One of the stories which has had a wholesome, liberating effect upon millions over centuries concerns the prophet Elijah, the great forerunner of John the Baptist and the one whom orthodox Jews today believe will return to herald the coming of Messiah. The Cup of Elijah is still a prominent feature of every Passover. In the New Testament account of the Transfiguration, it is Elijah who joins with Moses and Jesus on the mountaintop.

The context of the quotation that begins this section is this: the prophet has been waging a campaign against the fertility cult of the god Baal, whose chief champion is the ill-reputed Queen Jezebel. The queen's anger against Elijah reaches new heights after Elijah defeats the prophets of Baal in a kind of "Who's got the greatest god?" contest, and then has all her prophets killed (1 Kings 18:20–40). The queen sends a messenger to Elijah warning him that she plans to have him dispatched the following day. Elijah immediately panics, flees the scene and, leaving his manservant at Beersheba, journeys on alone for another 15 to 20 miles into the wilderness.

"And [he] came and sat down under a solitary broom tree. He asked that he might die: 'It is enough; for now, O Lord, take away my life, for I am no better than my ancestors.' Then he lay down under the broom tree and fell asleep…" (1 Kings 19:4ff).

Obviously, God's servant or not, Elijah was depressed. In fact he was so deeply depressed that he longed for death. He even prayed for death and tried to tell God how he had been treated by fate, fortune, and the Divine. You may never have been in such a torment of fear and frustration, but we all know people who have been. To feel there's no reason for living, to feel utterly "God-forsaken" and defeated, is the end product of a lifetime of stress for all too many people. Notice, however, a terribly important aspect of the text here. It contains absolutely no judgment or condemnation of Elijah for his state. Unlike the too-often judgmental elders and congregations of various faiths today, there is no condemnation of Elijah and of his clinical depression. Any question there is seems to concern what can be done to end it, or at least alleviate it.

Basically, God sees to it that Elijah is properly fed and that he gets a break and some vigorous exercise; he is told to get up and walk for 40 days and 40 nights (a highly symbolic biblical number, which is the number of years the Israelites spent in the wilderness after the Exodus from Egypt, and the number of days Jesus spent in the wilderness, where he was tempted, before beginning his ministry). Elijah's journey took him to Mount Horeb, otherwise known as Mount Sinai or "The Mountain of God." There, he came to a cave and spent the night. Then followed a fresh vision of his calling.

A still, small voice

The vision of Elijah (1 Kings 19:9b–12) belongs to everyone regardless of creed. Notice that it begins with a clear focusing and awareness of the realities of his situation. As we have seen before, we cannot respond spiritually or in any other way to a stressing situation without paying strict attention first and throughout to what is really going on. We don't know if "the word of the Lord" that comes to Elijah was an inner prompting, or a deep intuition, or whether there was in fact an apparent "voice." In any case, the key question posed was (and still is for each of us), "What are you doing here, Elijah?" (1 Kings 19:9).

I have found that if you are caught in a crisis of tension, pressure, or anxiety, or if you experience nagging moments of panic, you can help yourself begin to unravel the worst of it by asking yourself this question: What am I doing in this "place" of my life's journey? How did I get here and where did I make the wrong move, choice, utterance, or omission? Answering this question can be hard work and is not, of itself, an instant solution. (There are no push-button or easy answers in any case.) But, as Elijah found, facing the truth is the first step toward healing.

Here's the biblical account.

> *Then the word of the Lord came to him, saying, "What are you doing here, Elijah?" He answered, "I have been very jealous for the Lord, the God of hosts; for the Israelites have forsaken your covenant, thrown down your altars, and killed your prophets with the sword. I alone am left, and they are seeking my life, to take it away."*
>
> *He said, "Go out and stand on the mountain before the Lord, for the Lord is about to pass by."*
>
> *Now there was a great wind, so strong that it was splitting mountains and breaking rocks in pieces…but the Lord was not in the wind; and after the wind an earthquake, but the Lord was not in the earthquake; and after the earthquake a fire, but the Lord was not in the fire; and after the fire a sound of sheer silence.*

The King James Version at this point translates it as "and after the fire a still small voice" (1 Kings 19:12). The cosmic, Divine Presence made itself known in the sound of silence, a silence more eloquent, more searching, more healing than anything Elijah had ever known before.

Strikingly, the prophet then hears for a second time the great question – the one that makes so many of us twist and turn like a worm on a hook as we seek to avoid allowing ourselves to hear it: "What are you doing here, Elijah?" You can put your own name in the place of Elijah's at this juncture! The prophet still tries for a moment to fudge the issue by a tactic we all know well. He stalls by repeating his feeling-sorry-for-myself routine, wherein he complains about how he has done all kinds of things for the Lord and how he is the only faithful Israelite left, and yet his life is in danger (the life he was so keen not long before to get rid of!).

God, however, ignores his whining entirely, and gives him a fresh direction and task. At the same time, Elijah's illusion that he is completely on his own – the key temptation for millions in our overwrought, secular world – is totally smashed. The truth is that he is very far from alone. Not counting the ever-constant Divine Presence, there are, he is told, "several thousand" left in Israel who have not "bowed to Baal." Almost immediately, he meets and wins over Elisha, who will help him and then become his successor.

There is tremendous power in this timeless story. It is not about magical remedies or great piety. It's rooted in reality. It's about the stuff of life – strenuous exertion, fatigue, burnout, depression, and self-pity on the one hand; and renewed courage, illumination, and wholeness on the other. How does this renewal come? By hearing the heavenly voice within, by seeing the situation as it is, by challenging one's self-serving illusions, by finding fresh tasks to do, and by the renewed sense of others – a community – to serve and be with.

THE PSALMS

When one knows Thee, then alien is there none, then no door is shut.
O grant me my prayer that I may never lose the touch of
the One in the play of the many.
Rabindranath Tagore (1861–1941)

One of the most universally-loved sources of inspiration and courage for living a life that is more whole, caring, and calm, yet productive and vibrant as well, is the Psalter or Book of Psalms. Written over a considerable stretch of time by many different authors, beginning with King David himself who is credited with having written approximately half of the 150 psalms in the collection, this multi-faceted treasure belongs to all humanity. It will be kept and read as long as there are people anywhere on Earth – or as North American natives put it, as long as the sun rises or the rivers flow to the sea.

There are some genuinely problematic passages in a few of the psalms known as "the cursing psalms." There are also, however, a good many commentaries and studies that tackle these head-on and help, at least in most cases, to provide a reasonable explanation. C. S. Lewis' book *Reflections on the Psalms* is often recommended for this reason and for other reasons as well. For practical purposes, I have found that if you understand the surface violence or hatred expressed against the psalmist's "enemies" as an internal battle against the recurring habits of thinking and acting that cause us to be swamped by stress, even these cursing psalms can be very useful. It is sometimes calming and renewing to treat one's inner negative feelings or thoughts aggressively. Seeing them as enemies, or hating them, can "get it out there" and strengthen our will to change.

Here's a brief passage from Psalm 3, which illustrates the point. The writer begins, "O Lord, how many are my foes! Many are rising against me..." Then he cries, "Rise up, O Lord! Deliver me,

O my God! For you strike all my enemies on the cheek; you break the teeth of the wicked" (Psalm 3:7). Seen as imagery and metaphor – it is, after all, poetry – its meaning can be transformed. If this doesn't work for you, there are plenty of more positive assertions to be found, so one can just pass by the difficult verses.[3]

Here are some psalms and verses that can be used as mantras, for quiet repetition at any time of the day or night. If possible, breath slowly and deeply as you repeat them. There's no limit or minimum of how many to use, or for how long. I find it's best to expand according to the time available, instead of having a fixed rule. Incidentally, it's something many like to do while walking or traveling by plane, train, or car – provided they're not doing the driving. The precise references are given here and not as footnotes in order to simplify knowing the source in each case.

Good for periods of troubled sleep
I will both lie down and sleep in peace; for you alone,
O Lord, make me lie down in safety.
Psalm 4:8

For guidance when uncertain how to proceed
Lead me, O Lord, in your righteousness because of my enemies
[within or without]; make your way straight before me.
Psalm 5:8

For beginning a new day
Psalm 8 – In its totality, nine verses, it is a potent tool. It presents a vision of God that puts everything we are facing for the next 24 hours into a wholly fresh context – one that imbues all of our surroundings and our human condition itself with the Divine. It begins and ends with a refrain of praise and of seeing the whole of life *sub specie aeternitatis* – in the light of the Eternal. Put it on a tape for your car radio or for the bathroom as you get

ready for work. Or read it on the subway and again just before bed. It begins,

O Lord our Lord, how excellent is thy name in all the earth...
Psalm 8 (KJV)

An affirmation of fullness of life

You show me the path of life. In your presence there is fullness of joy; in your right hand are pleasures forevermore.
Psalm 16:11

This is what Dr. Larry Dossey, the well-known author and physician, calls "good medicine" for any phase of one's life. It's especially of help when black, negative thought patterns try to assert dominance over all else.

On gratitude

Psalm 18:1, 2 – One way to find strength and encouragement for life's darker moments or seasons is to be meticulous in giving thanks for all "mercies," particularly the small ones so often overlooked unless one strives to be aware. By thanking God, the universe, or our own grasp of the "Higher Power," we remain doubly sensitive to the positive aspects of our journey while reassuring our inner self that our spiritual path is being confirmed. What the Divine has done in the past it can still do in and for your life as you open up. Praise is always a sign of hope. Meister Eckhart says that the prayer of a simple "thanks" is really the only prayer we need.

The first two verses of Psalm 18 provide a base for this kind of meditation or prayer-affirmation:

I love you, O Lord, my strength. The Lord is my rock, my fortress, and my deliverer, my God, my rock in whom I take refuge, my shield, and the horn of my salvation, my stronghold.

On nature

The heavens declare the glory of God.

Psalm 19:1 (KJV)

The quiet contemplation of our natural surroundings in a garden, on holidays at a cottage, at the seaside, hiking in the hills
or mountains, or while scanning a star-filled sky at some spot
beyond city lights, has always – since our earliest memories –
soothed and calmed our stresses and our fears. Reading the
Bible or the sacred literature of other traditions reveals that
nature has always been the great teacher and the great healer
where stress is concerned. But not everyone notices how huge
a part it plays in shaping our sense of the spiritual itself, of the
inner and the eternal dimensions of life. What's more, it powerfully integrates us into the vast reaches and fabric of the
cosmos. It brings us a much-needed "belongingness" to our
environment, to our solar system, and to the spiralling galaxies
beyond. As noted before, Albert Einstein stressed several times
in his writings that we need to be drawn out far beyond the
cares and interests or pains of our own limited selves and into
the much larger reality of not just other people, but of the
universe in all its variety and grandeur. Part of our stress in the
modern world is caused by being locked so tightly into an
artificial habitat, where one can live a very lonely life in the
midst of teeming crowds and be cut off from his or her
rootedness in Mother Earth and all of creation.

Let me be personal. In my life spent studying religion, spirituality, and theology, or else reporting on it, nothing has ever
spoken to my heart, mind, and soul about ultimate things – about
God – in the way that the outdoors, the natural world, and
communing with animals, birds, flowing waters, forests, mountains, valleys, and winds have done.

Psalm 19 expresses this truth better than anyone can. It can
be used as contact point or an inner release when your job, your

social life, or your life in general make you feel intensely nervous or shut off from the joy and the energies that flow when one is connected with the natural whole. I am reminded of the lines by William Bliss Carman (1861–1929):

> *I took a day to search for God,*
> *And found Him not. But as I trod*
> *By rocky ledge, through woods untamed,*
> *Just where one scarlet lily flamed,*
> *I saw His footprint in the sod.*[4]

On the Divine Presence
The Lord is my shepherd,
I shall not want.

Psalm 23:1

I have written about this psalm elsewhere and will not repeat it here. But I know of few more insightful, therapeutic prayers/meditations than this. Often, while walking, or in sudden moments of stress, say before giving an address or an interview for the media, I find myself silently affirming and reaffirming part of verse 4. You could call it my "emergency mantra." In the King James Version it reads, "I will fear no evil: for thou art with me…" Often, I just use four words of this: "Thou art with me." The NRSV puts it less quaintly: "You are with me."

On wholeness and light
The Lord is my light and my wholeness, whom shall I fear.
The Lord is the powerhouse of my life,
of whom shall I be afraid?

(my own version)

The NRSV reads,

> *The Lord is my light and my salvation; whom shall I fear.*
> *The Lord is the stronghold of my life;*
> *of whom shall I be afraid?*
>
> Psalm 27:1

This verse and the last two verses of the psalm reaffirm in a most excellent way the power and illumination that is always available to us, even though at times we may have to "wait for the Lord." Once again, they have been an enormous help to me all my life. Millions could say, "Amen."

Here are the two verses from the end:

> *I believe that I shall see the goodness of the Lord in*
> *the land of the living. Wait for the Lord; be strong, and*
> *let your heart take courage; wait for the Lord!*

The "spring" of life within
For with you is the fountain of life; in your light we see light.

Psalm 36:9

However you define or think of God or the Divine within you, there are times of stress when to take even five or ten minutes to be still – even if you are walking you can be still at the center – and to silently say these words over and over again can make a difference. Once made into a habit, they can become an automatic part of your stress response. You'll be surprised at how they bring a sense of confidence that life energy is welling up inside. There's a growing feeling of calmness as the "light" begins to lift the mantle of darkness around you.

On trust
Psalm 37:3–7 – Some brief, mantra-like, spiritual advice:

Trust in the Lord, and do good; so you will dwell in the land and enjoy security. Take delight in the Lord, who will give you the desires of your heart. Commit your way to the Lord; trust in God and God will act...Be still before the Lord, and wait patiently for God...

Inclusive Language Psalms

The joy of release from deep stress

Psalm 40 – When you want and need to express your gratitude to God for experienced growth, relief, and healing, the first three verses of this psalm are invaluable:

I waited patiently for the Lord, who inclined to me and heard my cry. God drew me up from the desolate pit, out of the miry bog, and set my feet upon a rock, making my steps secure. God put a new song in my mouth, a song of praise to our God. Many will see and fear [have a deep sense of awe] and put their trust in the Lord.

A lesson in how to pray

Psalm 42 – Elsewhere, I have strongly emphasized the great importance of honesty and passion in praying. No other source states this truth more clearly than this psalm. Quietly affirming or praying it along with the psalmist can lift one out of negative feelings or patterns. Few words in the English language have more power to heal.

The words are very beautiful. For example, it begins,

As a deer longs for flowing streams, so my soul longs for you, O God. My soul thirsts for God, for the living God. When shall I come and behold the face of God?

The frankness is quite startling for any who suppose prayer to be some nice, pious and polite "conversation with God." For example, the author asks,

I say to God, my rock, "Why have you forgotten me?
Why must I walk about mournfully
because the enemy oppresses me?"

He faces the fact that he is depressed quite boldly, in verse 5:

Why are you cast down O my soul,
and why are you disquieted within me?

This question is repeated in the final verse of this very candid soul dialogue. But the psalmist answers it himself:

Hope in God; for I shall again praise the Lord,
my help and my God.

God as our refuge and strength

Psalm 46:1 – This psalm, upon which Martin Luther's famous hymn *A Mighty Fortress Is Our God* was based, is a classic Hebrew/Christian spiritual meditation. From it, in verse 10, comes one of the best-known sayings in the whole of scripture: "Be still, and know that I am God."

The entire poem is a bracing tonic for those times when we feel weak and afraid. It deserves to be run in full, but I leave it to you to look it up for yourself.

Here is the first verse and part of the next, to be used on their own as a foundation for a quiet preparation for any scenario:

God is our refuge and strength, a very present help in trouble.
Therefore we will not fear, though the earth should change,
though the mountains shake...

On forgiveness

Psalm 51 – This entire psalm is dubbed a "prayer for cleansing and pardon," by the editors of the NRSV. It is believed to have been written by King David after his adultery with Bathsheba and his successful plot to murder her husband by putting him in the front lines of battle and then having the soldiers close to him leave him exposed.

There are times when the weight of stress can warp our judgment and cause us to do things we normally would never consider. Substance abuse, angry quarrels, violence – any one of a thousand behavioral problems and the unhappiness surrounding them – are flowing today from daily stress that for millions has become out of control. One highly significant aspect of the healing process which must take place is often left out – true contrition and forgiveness. Forgiveness from those injured most, from the mystery we name God, and last but not least, from ourselves.

This psalm can be a healthy, positive tool in any recovery. I give only the first two verses; they are enough. But once again I urge you to get a copy of the Psalms and read Psalm 51 in its entirety:

Have mercy on me, O God, according to your steadfast love;
according to your abundant mercy blot out my transgressions.
Wash me thoroughly from my iniquity, and cleanse me from my sin.

To be truly repentant, to make adequate and appropriate reparations before God, is to be forgiven. No priest, minister, or other agent of religion is required unless further assurance or a deeper understanding of one's problems is needed. Then, of course, whatever profession (be it medical, psychiatric, or ministerial) seems most suitable should be consulted.

Summary

Again, there is much more that could be said. The Psalms, as a book, can never be exhausted by any soul that is truly searching for more light and more strength for the journey. Psalm 91, for example, is a much-beloved meditation for encouragement; Psalm 103 is a priceless, liberating song of thanksgiving for persons of nearly all religious backgrounds and of none; Psalm 121, which begins, "I lift up my eyes to the hills – from where will my help come?" is another world favorite; and Psalm 139, which speaks so movingly of the inescapability of God, of God's marvelous love for us no matter where we go, literally or metaphorically, is my personal favorite.

But you can and will find others, too, once you open the Psalter in this way. It's a lifelong exploration, once you see yourself as the person to whom the truths revealed in the psalms are really being addressed.

There are, as I've already said, 150 psalms. It's interesting, I believe, that the 150th ends with these words:

Let everything that breathes praise the Lord! Praise the Lord!

This is an affirmation that the spiritual heart is one that inwardly thanks God, with every breath, for this moment, for life, for creation, and for all that is wholesome and good. Our breath, so often ignored, is the most spiritual tool of them all.

THE BOOK OF PROVERBS

Wisdom, a sense of security, and a long life

One thing I have noticed over many years is that spiritually inclined people seldom pray for wisdom. They ask for everything else – material things, health, spiritual progress, and much more. But wisdom, understanding, and insight come far down the list, if they're there at all. This is a great loss in general, but particularly when we're responding to the stresses and excessive tensions of living in today's dangerous and hectic world. There can be little personal transformation without the presence and grace of wisdom.

The Book of Proverbs, mostly but not all attributable to King Solomon (in the tenth century BCE), is a practical, yet at times lyrical call to seek after wisdom and to realize that at its very heart lies a deep and abiding trust in the divine wisdom of God. Notice that as in classical Greek thinking, where the word is Sophia, the ancient Hebrews thought of wisdom as feminine.

There are so many positive and comforting insights contained in Proverbs that one should read the entire book. But I offer here, as a tested source for meditation and inspiration, simply a few lines from Proverbs, chapter three. They are timeless food for the soul, an infinite healing for the mind and heart.

True wealth

Happy are those who find wisdom,
and those who get understanding,
for her income is better than silver,
and her revenue better than gold.
She is more precious than jewels,
and nothing you desire can compare with her.
Long life is in her right hand;
in her left hand are riches and honor.
Her ways are ways of pleasantness,
and all her paths are peace.
She is a tree of life to those who lay hold of her;
those who hold her fast are called happy.
Proverbs 3:11–18

God's wisdom in creation
The Lord by wisdom founded the earth;
by understanding God established the heavens;
by God's knowledge the deeps broke open,
and the clouds drop down the dew.
Proverbs 3:19–20

True Security
My child, do not let these escape from your sight:
keep sound wisdom and prudence,
and they will be life for your soul
and adornment for your neck.
Then you will walk on your way securely
and your foot will not stumble.
If you sit down, you will not be afraid;
when you lie down, your sleep will be sweet.
Do not be afraid of sudden panic,
or of the storm that strikes the wicked;
for the Lord will be your confidence
and will keep your foot from being caught.
Proverbs 3:21–26

Once again, one cannot even attempt to cover it all. The remaining books of the Old Testament, especially Isaiah, resound with encouragement and strength for all those yearning for a deeper, more spiritual path as they learn to live more creatively with stress. I would like in particular to draw your attention to such famous passages as the whole of Isaiah chapter 40, and chapters 41:8–10, and 61:1–4.

But it's time now to turn briefly to the New Testament and to set forth at least some of the riches there.

IX

FROM
THE NEW TESTAMENT

Jesus says:
"Where there are two, they are not without God.
Where there is one, I say that I am with him. Pick up a stone,
There (in it?) you will find me.
Cut wood in two, I am also there.
Where two are together, God is there.
If only one is there, he is not without the presence of Christ.
The trees speak of his presence.
The rocks echo that voice."
Oxyrhynchus Papyrus #1[1]

Because the New Testament is probably more familiar to most of the readers of this book – believers or not – than the Hebrew Bible or Old Testament, I don't propose to set out more than a small sampling of the plethora of passages and sayings relating to our theme. Those passages I have included were chosen after considerable reflection and, in most cases, as a result of a history of personal use by myself and by millions of Christ's followers over the course of time. They are aimed directly at anxiety, worry, depression, and stress. As far as possible, I intend to avoid here all matters relating to formal theology, Bible criticism, or textual problems. Discussion of these things belongs to a later part of the book. In any case, good commentaries are now available at libraries and bookstores everywhere.

THE GOSPELS

One thing all four gospels agree upon: Jesus was strongly interested in the sufferings of other human beings and did everything in his power to bring about healing. He was someone through whom healing energy and healing words flowed from the Source of Life itself. He proclaimed the Kingdom of God (God's ruling presence) and manifested it through his own life and mission.

Fully human himself, though filled by the Divine Spirit, Jesus knew firsthand what care, pressure, and stress are about. As the author of Hebrews says, "we have one who in every respect has been tested as we are..."

MATTHEW'S GOSPEL

The Beatitudes, which begin the Sermon on the Mount in Matthew, chapters 5–7, read as follows:

Blessed are the poor in spirit,
for theirs is the Kingdom of Heaven.
Blessed are those who mourn,
for they will be comforted.
Blessed are the meek,
for they will inherit the earth.
Blessed are those who hunger and thirst
for righteousness, for they will be filled.
Blessed are the merciful,
for they will receive mercy.

Blessed are the pure in heart,
for they will see God.
Blessed are the peacemakers,
for they will be called the children of God.
Blessed are those who are persecuted for righteousness sake,
for theirs is the Kingdom of Heaven.

This passage, like the weather, is much-talked about, but, as Mark Twain remarked, "Nobody does much about it." In other words, the full impact of these words tends to get lost in a mist of sentimentality. These sayings, beginning with the words, "Blessed are…" (the modern equivalent is really, "Hearty congratulations to you if you are…") represent a total reversal of the kind of values and standards that produce so much of the stress endured by contemporary men and women. What are our popular values? Success and always being on top; health and happiness; celebrity, with all its glitter; wealth and the show of riches; getting your own dues and rights; popularity and being one of the "gang"; assertiveness and attractiveness; and all the rest.

The words of Jesus here are stunning compared with these current views. They stand each of these values on its head and instead pronounce as "blessed" or "congratulated" those who are humble, in grief, persecuted, single in heart (about serving God and others), and seekers after peace. They offer a unique chance to take another look at our lives and ask how much of the anxiety and stress we experience comes from our conformity to society's norms, our own ambitions and the lust to grasp at material "success." Envy of others who are more successful than we are, better looking, or whatever, can cause enormous strain. So, too, can the ever-present sense of never being satisfied, of never getting enough – praise, money, honors, or things. In Buddhism, this kind of "attachment" to fleeting illusions is considered to be the chief source of human misery.

Love of enemies?

Like many, I know that whatever else I am, I'm a news addict. It can become a near-vice. On the other hand, there's no virtue in arbitrarily refusing to pay attention to what's going on around us.

Those who in the name of a higher spirituality make themselves blind and deaf to the glories, follies, and tragedies of the global village – reported in the media – risk losing their souls in a hell of isolation and selfishness. But as we read our newspaper or watch BBC World News, CNN, or listen to CBC Radio, and try our best to be aware and informed, there are soul risks too. The greatest risk is that of being so flooded by the torrent of information that we ignore the much profounder issues behind the day's or the week's events. We ignore the spiritual subtext. Thus, for example, it's easier to ponder a future with George W. Bush trying to call the shots on everything from biological warfare to the environment, especially in this new era of the "War on Terror," or to file away how many more Palestinians or Israelis have been killed in what can surely no longer be called "The Holy Land," than it is to think about the fundamental causes of violence and discord.

We forget that the global picture is a projection on a large scale of what goes on inside every human being's own heart. Every truly inspired prophet, poet, and visionary, has made it plain that both the cause and the solution of every human problem, whatever its scale might be, lie in the heart and mind of each individual member of our species. The spiritual giants throughout all time make it clear; if we want a world free of hatred, greed, and injustice, we must begin by clearing our own inner lives of enmity, hate, graspingness, and the condoning of injustices, however small, which secretly benefit us. This is hard soul-work and requires fervent prayer as we do our part.

One of the most powerful visions of how this can happen comes from the most original – and most challenging – pronouncement of Jesus, in the balance of The Sermon on the Mount where he boldly commands us to "love our enemies."[2]

Yes, we've heard those words before. But take a few moments and really let them sink in. Never in the history of the world has a radical moral principle been formed and enunciated more clearly or potently than this. Yet, never, in all the centuries since, has humanity rejected any commandment, principle, or rule more fully – even more enthusiastically – than this. To have even mentioned it with regard to Osama Bin Laden, say, or to the Taliban and the web of terrorists associated with them, in the months immediately following September 11, 2001, would have been to invite ridicule or much worse!

One is reminded of G. K. Chesterton's insight: "The Christian ideal has not been tried and found wanting. It has been found difficult, and left untried."

Certainly, Christians have never been found leading the charge, so to speak, when love of enemies has been required – with the possible exception of the Quakers and Mennonites. From my long familiarity with the many tensions in local congregations and with all that goes under the general tab of "church politics," it seems indeed that many would-be Christians have a tough enough time trying to love their friends never mind possible foes!

This is far from a light matter, however. News items about road rage, airline passenger rage, and domestic or other forms of societal rage – for example, the ongoing race riots in England's industrial north at the time of writing – all reveal that there is often a seething cauldron of hate at the heart level that sooner or later gets acted out collectively in vaster arenas.

There are two things to remember in connection to this. The first is that in saying we should love and not hate our enemies, Christ was aware that there is a powerful spiritual law according to which we tend to become like the object we hate. In other words, one must be careful whom or what he/she hates,

136 ᚱ FINDING THE STILL POINT

because somehow, in this hot fixation of emotions, the hatred recoils on the hater.

The second is that the Greek word for "love" of enemies is the same word the New Testament uses for love of God and love of neighbor. It doesn't mean anything mushy or sentimental. It has to do with respecting and willing the very best for the "other." To love either your neighbor or your enemy in this sense doesn't mean you necessarily have to like them.

Jesus doesn't say, "Like your enemies...pray for your persecutors." He says, "Get rid of the hatred; wish for them what you wish for yourself; pray for true repentance for both parties." As we absorb the daily news, we often wish we could change the world. We *can*, by beginning at home.

Carl Jung once wrote, at the height (or perhaps we should say depth) of the Cold War, that it would take only the slightest change in the stability of the minds of the world leaders with access to the "nuclear button" to plunge the world into chaos and annihilation. His saying can be reversed. It would take only a slight change in the minds and hearts of Earth's billions of people to shift the balance towards global peace, justice, and ecological renewal. That's what spiritual renewal is about.

Apart from all of that, we lose an incredible amount of energy whenever we give root to dislike, malice, hatred, or sheer enmity against someone. It drains away energy that should be available for living and loving, while making us miserable at the same time. I remember well doing an hour-long TV interview with a distinguished Canadian priest who had survived an impressive number of years with a malignant, purportedly fatal tumor in his brain. His name was Bob Ogle. He was from western Canada and he served as a Member of Parliament for several years until Pope John Paul II ordered him to get out of politics. In the course of the show, Ogle described what it was like going home on a streetcar through downtown Toronto after learning of his diagnosis – the feeling of looking out at all that life and feeling nothing but blank despair.

However, he also described how he soon decided to rise above his self-pity and depression and to make sense of life as he struggled to meet the challenge. What stood out for me – especially when he went on to live productively for many years – was his decision immediately to draw up a list of all his "enemies" and to make things right with them. He told me, "I knew I should do that as a Christian. But, to tell the truth, a person only has so much energy flowing into and through him or her. I can't afford leakage from being at odds with others. I need all the energy I can get to help my body cope with cancer."

Jesus' principle of loving (not hating) our enemies is not an idealistic piece of piety, but a most practical prescription for spiritual and physical health.[3]

Worry or moment-by-moment mindfulness?

There are frequent warnings throughout the New Testament about the harm and waste of energy caused by worrying. The method it recommends for dealing with it is not the simple – and to be truthful – unhelpful, even useless suggestion to "just stop doing it." That, as everyone knows, is not what is needed or wanted. It's like telling a depressed person to smile and look on the bright side.

In the Sermon on the Mount, in the chapter following the words about enemies, Jesus comments on how a different perspective can remove most worry (Matthew 6:25ff). God knows we have legitimate needs, but, Jesus says, "Strive first for the Kingdom of God [God's supremacy in all things] and all these things will be given you." In particular, he urges his audience (and us), to practice moment-by-moment mindfulness. Live in the moment, he says (as do teachers of modern mindfulness meditation), and you'll be so aware of the present as to leave for the future its own space when it comes: "So do not worry about tomorrow, for tomorrow will bring worries of its own. Today's trouble is enough for today" (Matthew 6:34).

Release from stress

"Come to me, all you that are weary and are carrying heavy burdens, and I will give you rest. Take my yoke [or yoga] upon you, and learn from me; for I am gentle and humble in heart, and you will find rest for your souls. For my yoke is easy, and my burden light" (Matthew 11:28–30).

This remarkable appeal, directly aimed at all the stressed and straining masses of humanity, then and to come, is well-known to Christians and others with any familiarity with the historic Anglican Church's *Book of Common Prayer*. It constitutes an intimate part of the Service of Holy Communion known as "The Comfortable Words."

While obviously meant for Christians particularly, the words are, nevertheless, worth reading and pondering by outsiders of all kinds. "Weary and carrying heavy burdens" is an apt description of those who have been close to or who are presently experiencing "burnout" from chronic stress. Jesus promises that there can be rest, release, and renewal from such a weight of fatigue and care. By inviting all to "take my yoke upon you," he means that his gentle teaching and example – his yoga, for the Greek word as we've already seen means that, just as the Sanskrit word "yoga" means yoke – are a path to inner peace. Notice he rightly sees the stressed person's need as a "rest" for the soul. His yoga, or yoke, joining the spiritual and the body-mind is "easy"; it doesn't chafe, and the "burden" of discipleship is "light." This invitation, in this context, is not about becoming a card-carrying, creed-believing Christian, or "born again"; it's about a tried and proven way of responding to a critical issue for all time, but especially right now. Too many of us Christians have heard these phrases ten thousand times and yet have never really *listened* to them once.

Some loose ends. These could have been left to the end of our scanning of all four gospels, but this seems to me a better place to pull them together.

Walking the talk

Jesus' actions are in complete accord with his words. He walks – and lives – the talk. This comes home to me every time I read Matthew's account of the storm on the Sea of Galilee and how, in spite of the tossing boat, Jesus was quietly asleep in the stern through it all. Whatever critics may make of the miracle of stilling the storm itself, such a detail of description strikes this writer's eye with the note of authority and truth. Jesus was taking a necessary break as part of properly caring for his own body and health. And he could relax enough to do it. To be able to do that in the face of stress means you have often done it when things were much more serene.

On being kind to yourself

Not just in Matthew but in all the gospels we see a profound rhythm at the heart of Jesus' own lifestyle or *modus vivendi* (quite literally). His pattern was one of regularly seeking out solitude, particularly at dawn or even earlier, for meditation and prayer. His ministry is marked by periods of extreme busyness, being constantly jostled by crowds, relentlessly sought out by the sick and needy, and frequently needled by his often thick-witted, contentious disciples. In the background, there is always a growing sense of being a marked man, destined to be done away with. Nevertheless, Jesus makes it a priority to take times of rest, to escape the throng, and to be alone with nature. He observed the Sabbath even though he deepened its meaning with his famous saying that people were not made for the Sabbath, but the Sabbath for people.

Jesus was unlike many Christians I knew in my youth for whom the seventh day was a ceaseless, nerve-wracking to-and-fro-ing from church. He attended the synagogue and sometimes this got him into trouble, but the general picture we have is that he used it for a time of reflection and rest. In our family when I was growing up, my father was always a Sunday school superintendent, heavily dependent on the rest of us to assist by teaching, playing the piano, and, in my mother's case, by being organizer and trouble-shooter par excellence. He ran great Sunday schools. We went to church three times on Sunday, often having lunch in the kitchen there. Yet it was hectic and stressful since we lived in the east end of Toronto and yet attended a church right down-town. The weariness and fractiousness engendered by it all was sometimes far from the internal peace and quiet originally in-tended.

In the Genesis myth of Creation, we are told how God "rested" on the seventh day. It hardly needs saying that this is not meant as anything remotely historical or literal. It simply lays down an eternal principle. First, creativity and work, then a re-newing pause. There is a kind of religion which hears the first part but feels guilty about rest or proper self-care. Greater stress is inevitably the result. The secret of Jesus' serenity and calmness throughout his life, and especially when faced with torture and the cruellest of deaths, lies deep in the balance he had deter-mined for himself from his early boyhood. Having proper relax-ation and rest is as important a part of spiritual discipline as meditation or work.

LUKE'S GOSPEL

Luke, we know, like Matthew, had a copy of Mark's gospel in front of him as he wrote. Also, he had a document – a written source of sayings (no Passion or Resurrection story, just a col-lection of remembered *logia*, or sayings, called "Q," from the German word for source, *Quelle*). But, also like Matthew, Luke had in addition a separate oral or written source of his own with some unique material not found in any other gospel. Scholars call this source "L." Matthew's special source is called "M."

So, as we would thus conclude, Mark is common to all the first three gospels, the "synoptics." But there is much in Luke that is identical with or like a paraphrase of Matthew. Yet there are also original, fresh verses too. This will become clear in the four Lucan words and events we look at now.

Words for the weary and oppressed

In Luke 4:16ff there is a story, found also in Mark and Matthew, about Jesus being rejected at the synagogue in his hometown of Nazareth. But only Luke, using "L," tells us what Jesus preached about and how he applied it. His commentary, verses 18–19, summarizes what Luke believes is Jesus' entire platform or message. I include it here because people are confused about what Jesus stands for and about what his message is. According to Luke, Jesus' ministry, life, death, and resurrection were on behalf of human liberation.

He stood up to read and the scroll of the prophet Isaiah was given to him. He unrolled the scroll and found the place where it was written:

> *The Spirit of the Lord is upon me,*
> *because he has anointed me*
> *to bring good news to the poor.*
> *He has sent me to proclaim*
> *release to the captives*
> *and recovery of sight to the blind,*
> *to let the oppressed go free,*
> *to proclaim the year of the Lord's favor.*

Then he concluded by saying, "Today this scripture has been fulfilled in your hearing." After a short time of discussion and some amazement, the congregation became enraged and drove him out of town.

Jesus, then, saw himself as anointed by the Spirit of God to point the way to freedom for real living. Read spiritually, he's talking about a goal espoused both by secular humanists today and by believers of every kind – the full realization of the emancipation of every human being: good news for the poor, that is, justice and relief; liberty to all those held captive by political forces or by fears, anxieties, pressures, worries, and pain; spiritual sight to those who cannot yet see where their highest good lies or the resources within and without for coping with and over-coming their limitations; and to let those oppressed (the Greek says the "worn down," the "broken down," or the "crushed" – as in what we call a "breakdown") by life's stresses, go free.

To proclaim the year of the Lord's favor, the phrase with which the passage concludes, means to announce that the time of God's favor towards us is right now, this year, this week, this day, at this very moment. Read slowly, with deep breathing, this can be a positive antidote to negative, dark thoughts and outlook.

Incidentally, the devout in the synagogue were not upset by his aims; they were furious at the authoritative way he claimed Isaiah's promises were being brought to pass by him, a home-town boy from their own remote, small village in the Galilee.

Reducing stress through right action

The sayings and the rest of the tradition directly bearing on Jesus' moral teaching come partly from their common non-Marcan source, Q, and partly in each case from their own singu-lar source: "L" in the case of Luke, "M" in the case of Matthew. So, while Mark has no Sermon on the Mount at all, Matthew and Luke have their own particular versions. For example, Matthew's sermon is indeed from a mountainside – though like those readers who have been there, I remember it as somewhat less than a hill; Luke's sermon takes place on a plain. Luke says, in fact, "He came down with them and stood on a level place…Then he looked up at his disciples and said:

Blessed are you who are poor…
Luke 6:17–49

Integral to both accounts is an aspect I deliberately passed over when dealing with the Beatitudes earlier. I'm referring to the warnings about being judgmental and prone to condemnation of people, places, situations, or other pet hates. The more you study the spiritual texts of all major faiths, the more you read contemporary spiritual leaders and interpreters of today, the more astonishing the unity between them all on this specific point becomes. Everyone who knows anything about the soul and its health, and particularly about the effects of a well or sick soul upon the mind and the body, stresses this same truth: to be well and at peace, stop all judging of others and put an end to the spirit of condemnation that can possess a person's total outlook. Like it or not, judging is bad, even ruinous. It can wither others. It can destroy oneself.

It's enormously therapeutic, when struggling to respond better to stress, to do a spiritual self-examination. Luke's account of what Jesus had to say about judging can be used as a standard and guide.

Do not judge, and you will not be judged; do not condemn, and you will not be condemned. Forgive, and you will be forgiven; give, and it will be given unto you. A good measure, pressed down, shaken together, running over, will be put into your lap; for the measure you give will be the measure you get back.

Luke 6:37–38

There is more wholeness, more tension release, more health in the repetition and constant implementation of the above few lines than in a dozen of any of the expensive wonder-mixes, herbs, juices, or medicines people flock to buy at whatever price or to obtain from their doctors. Experiment yourself and see.

Greed and acquisitiveness as triggers of stress

We listed earlier a number of reasons why people today are experiencing stresses far in excess of those our spirit-mind-body organisms were ever intended to endure. Jesus identifies over-anxiety about both the necessities and the luxuries "out there" – an obsession with having more – as an often-overlooked key cause of such extra strain. What would he say were he to walk the streets of the so-called developed countries today? Our whole lives, our economies in our part of the world run solely on commercialism – the buying and selling of ever-multiplying things. Being a "consumer" is the chief mode of showing you are a good citizen. A massive bombardment of advertising constantly urges us to buy and get more. Our children are targeted as a highly effective means to ensure the whole process has a future.

Luke's Jesus has a sharp, counterculture rebuke for that:

> *Take care! Be on your guard against all kinds of greed; for one's life*
> *does not consist in the abundance of possessions.*
> Luke 12:13ff

Of course, we all have legitimate needs that enable us to live productive, happy lives. But everybody in the Western world knows we have too much – far, far too much. What's more, this grasping is killing us with its rush to keep up to the neighbors, its pressure to eat more and drink more, to climb a corporate or other ladder, to buy this model car or that home with the three-car garage. This saying, together with the short parable that follows it, Luke 12:16–21, can cut off or help us avoid a lot of unbearable stress once we apply it to ourselves. Some stresses cannot be avoided, but the incredible stress due to greed, over-ambition, and pressures to "get to the top" by climbing over everybody else, can and must be dealt with if we truly desire peace within.

Infinite possibilities

One of the most attractive and potent aspects of Dr. Deepak Chopra's popular writings is the emphasis he makes upon the belief that, with God, all things are possible. That he does this most often by comparing spiritual truths with the amazing insights of modern quantum physics serves to make this teaching even more appealing. In all of his recent books, most especially in *How to Know God*, he points out how the cosmos is indeed a world of all possibilities; what he calls "infinite possibility, infinite creativity, infinite wisdom," and much more. Creation out of the quantum sea of pure potential goes on nanosecond by nanosecond. Through the creative use of mind and thought, we can ourselves manifest today what was only a possibility yesterday.

While not using the terminology of physics, the New Testament also enunciates exactly what Chopra is speaking about. In many places it states unequivocally that "with God, nothing is impossible," or that "with God, all things are possible." In the gospels, Jesus both states and lives such a belief. For example, in Luke 18:26 he remarked, "What is impossible for mortals is possible for God." In Mark 9:23 (KJV), Jesus says, "All things are possible to him that believeth." In the Lucan narrative just mentioned, Jesus had been commenting on just how difficult it is for those with great riches to enter the Kingdom of God. Members of the crowd immediately wanted to know, "Who then can be saved?" Hence his assurance that God's power is always available and is infinite in scope. Human impossibilities become divine opportunities. The repetition of "all things are possible" as a daily mantra is a powerful weapon when one feels weak, uncertain, upset, or even defeated by life's vicissitudes.

This is not the place for a cerebral discussion of miracles. It is sufficient for now to underline the truth known by all who have been and are striving to live life on a spiritual plane: there is an infinite strength and enabling power available to those who earnestly seek it out and ask for it. The success of Alcoholics Anonymous where all other means of curing this addiction have failed itself stands as a strong witness. Recovery programs of all kinds that leave out the spiritual side about forgiveness and about trust in a higher power, both within and without, have nowhere near the same effectiveness or results.

JOHN'S GOSPEL

Many hundreds, probably thousands even, of books have been written about John, the fourth gospel. That it was quite different from the other three gospels, the synoptics as they are called because they can be put side by side and one can see the obvious Marcan outline in each, was noticed by commentators as early as the second century CE. In general, it has been called "the spiritual gospel," because of its high view of Jesus' role as "God-in-the-flesh," and because of the various extensive – and unique – dialogues where the deep things of the Spirit are discussed.[4]

One thing is certain; the author, probably the apostle John, who was, as the text itself says, "the disciple whom Jesus loved," tells his readers quite explicitly in chapter 20:30–31 that he edited his material thoroughly to attempt to make converts:

> *Now Jesus did many other signs in the presence of his disciples, which are not written in this book. But these are written that you may come to believe that Jesus is the Messiah, the Son of God, and that through believing you might have life in his name.*

But, with that brief introduction, my aim once again is to offer some passages which throw light on or reinforce the spiritual aspirations of *all* people whether Christian-oriented or not. The more you study world religions, the more you become aware that, at their heart where ultimacies count, they nearly always – amazingly – speak with one voice.

On being born from above

The born-again movement in contemporary Christianity, indeed the phrase "born again" itself, derives essentially from John 3:13 and a somewhat arbitrary translation of one Greek word, *anothen* (ανωθεν). It can mean "from above" or "anew/again" and the latter is the choice of the King James Version (1611). However, the widely acclaimed, widely used New Revised Standard Version, translated about 400 years later (1993), but from much earlier manuscripts and in the light of a much vaster knowledge of how Hellenistic Greek words were used (from hoards of papyri discovered since the end of World War II in the sands of Egypt, from the Dead Sea Scrolls, the library at Nag Hammadhi, and many other places in the Middle East) translates ανωθεν, or *anothen*, as "*born from above.*" In other words, it follows the basic meaning of the term.

This radically affects this key Johannine passage which deals with the universal truth of our need, as spiritual beings, to have our spiritual nature touched, breathed upon, or released, however one wants to express it, *from above*, that is, from God, or Spirit Itself. Unfortunately, misuse and abuse of the words "born again" in the King James Version of John 3:3ff by various fundamentalist groups have made most ordinary people totally suspicious of the phrase itself and have thus kept them ignorant of the true concepts behind it.

Here is the story itself.

Now there was a Pharisee named Nicodemus, a leader of the Jews. [His Greek name means, in fact, a leader of the demos or people.] He came to Jesus by night and said to him, "Rabbi, we know that you are a teacher who has come from God"...Jesus answered him, "Very truly, I tell you, no one can see the kingdom of God [the kingdom of right relationships and of inner serenity] without being born from above."

Nicodemus said to him, "How can anyone be born after having grown old? Can one enter a second time into the mother's womb and be born?" Jesus answered, "Very truly, I tell you, no one can enter the kingdom of God without being born of water [the water of baptism or, much more likely in this context, the water of a natural birth] and Spirit. What is born of the flesh is flesh, and what is born of the Spirit is spirit. Do not be astonished that I said to you, 'You must be born from above.' The wind [pneuma, using the same Greek word as for Spirit] blows where it chooses, and you hear the sound of it, but you do not know where it comes from or where it goes. So it is with everyone who is born of the Spirit." [He means the same thing as "born from above."]

This truth is of great significance for anyone seeking a spiritual approach to anything, be it stress, pain, big decisions, or problems of whatever kind. John's Jesus says that to be spiritual at all means to believe in and know the reality being spoken of by Jesus here. In other words, one must grasp the truth that we are spiritual hominids. Our true spiritual self within needs to be realized or acknowledged or awakened "from above by God." It is in that light, as children of God, that our stresses and fears are to be responded to and transformed into energies for creativity and joy.

The Spirit alone gives life

Jesus said, "It is the spirit that gives life; the flesh [of itself alone] is useless. The words that I have spoken to you are spirit and life" (John 6:63).

One is instantly reminded of the words of the apostle Paul: "For the letter [a literal, legalistic understanding of sacred scriptures] kills, but the Spirit gives life" (2 Corinthians 3:6).

The 11th commandment

During the late 1950s and early 1960s, churches and denominations across North America were rapidly expanding into the growing suburbs of all major towns and cities. It was a time of unprecedented "church extension," as it was called. Young clergy such as myself were caught up in leading congregations to new building projects. At meetings we would joke together about a new, 11th commandment: "Thou shalt get thy congregation deeply in debt." But there was and is already an 11th commandment established and in place. It suffers, alas, from less observance than the quip about getting churches into debt.

Here it is from John 13:34.

> [Jesus said] "I give you a new commandment, that you love one another. Just as I have loved you, you also should love one another. By this everyone will know that you are my disciples, if you have love for one another."

In his famous poem "Leaves of Grass," Walt Whitman exults that in the end, "the kelson of creation is love." The word kelson denotes the part of a wooden ship where the keel meets the timbers tying in the main hull to this foundational point. The Concise Oxford dictionary, 1911, says, "The line of timber fastening ship's floor-timbers to keel." Whitman, who had seen a lot of the pain and suffering of the "real" world, was not alone in such a faith. Spiritual masters from every corner of the Earth have believed and taught the same. Those who know the millennia-old, Hindu Lovingkindness Meditation – in all its variations – know that Eastern spirituality was focused upon love, lovingkindness, or compassion, from very earliest times, certainly several thousand years before the birth of Christ.

So Jesus here sounds a universal truth. Our spiritual lives are often so anemic and faltering because we have taken such talk for granted for so long. To love one another is not a matter of mustering sentimental or emotional feelings for everybody we meet or know. It's simple, practical, and solid. It means strongly willing the very best – the kind of thing or life we want for ourselves – for all others around us and far away too. It's compassion for, as the Buddhists put it, "All sentient beings."

Praying daily for this kind of love and willing it, sending it forth with the breath, or in prayer, living it and letting it shine out of your eyes and out of your every action, is a way of simultaneously taking your thoughts and concerns away from stress while absorbing fresh energy for living to the full in the moment at hand.

The universal spirit

In one of my earlier books, I put forward and defended the thesis that the reason Jesus made such an incredible impression on his followers and then on the world was not that he was actually God walking about disguised as a human being. Rather, he was one who was filled with the Spirit of God beyond the limits previously known to or attained by us. He had opened his total being to God and lived in the constant awareness of his unity – a unity open to us all – with the divine mystery, whom he called "Father."

The emphasis on the Spirit (God active and present) is common to all religions – with the possible exception of strict Buddhism, and even there, semantics is often the main problem in trying to draw parallels. It is common to all indigenous peoples the world over, whether one is speaking of the *mana* of the Polynesians, the *Qi* (pronounced chee) of Chinese and Japanese ancient tradition, the *Atman* of Hinduism, the Great Spirit of the North American natives, or the light and fire symbolism of Zoroastrianism.

In Christianity, in both the Old and the New Testaments, the term Spirit flows throughout the text. As already remarked, the same word – pneuma in Greek and ruach in Hebrew – means wind and breath, and also the "Breath of God." Since the Book of Acts shows how the Spirit renewed and empowered the earliest Christians, it has often been called the Acts of the Holy Spirit.

Certainly the New Testament, when it speaks of Spirit, is specifically talking about a Divine Power that is understood (naturally) in terms of the nature and character of Jesus himself. It is the Spirit that possessed him and that he, in God's name, "gave" to the church. But non-Christians should remember that there is no way that any group or faith or institution has God's active power and "Being" wrapped up for themselves or privatized wholly for their sole use. Neither does any group have a monopolistic authority to dispense it – through clergy, rites, sacraments, or anything else. When God's Spirit is being spoken of, when God's Spirit is at work, when God's Spirit is prayed for sincerely, there are no divisions and no favorites.

So in listing some of the main references to the Spirit, our chief resource in finding strength for the fray and the serenity to bear all necessary stress, my intention is for all to partake. Devout Christians will read the texts slightly differently *but not with regard to the essentials* being conveyed. May I suggest having a Bible, preferably The New Revised Standard Version (NRSV), at hand while reading this brief section.

THE ACTS OF THE APOSTLES

The promise of the Spirit (Acts 1:4–5)
For a somewhat different version, see John 20:21–23.

The "birthday" of the Christian church (Acts 2:1–13)

Note that the whole "Jesus event" is symbolically portrayed here as releasing a vast charge of energy. New ideas and happenings on this scale inevitably have the power to overturn the past. It's not that no one had the spirit within them before Pentecost. Rather, it's a testimony to the arrival of an entirely fresh awareness of God's presence in their midst – a change of consciousness.

On being filled with the Spirit

Then Peter, filled with the Holy Spirit…

Acts 4:8

This is the keynote theme. The person seeking a truly spiritual response to life seeks first to be "filled" with the empowering, inner presence of Spirit.

Facing threats and danger

When they had prayed, the place in which they were gathered together was shaken; and they were all filled with the Holy Spirit and spoke the word of God with boldness.

Acts 4:31

Healing follows

A great number of people would also gather from the towns around Jerusalem, bringing the sick and those tormented by unclean spirits [emotional and mental ailments], and they were all cured.

Acts 5:12–16

Nobody excluded

While Peter was still speaking, the Holy Spirit fell upon all who heard the word. The circumcised [i.e., Jewish converts]… were astounded that the gift of the Holy Spirit had been poured out even on the Gentiles…

Acts 10:44–48

Peter then notes that nobody can prevent these Gentiles being baptized into full membership since they "have received the Holy Spirit just as we have."

Summary of Acts

There is as always so much more, particularly Luke's account of Paul's visit to Athens where, recognizing that such an audience required a very different approach, the apostle quotes their own poets to them and takes as his text an inscription from a nearby pagan altar: "To the Unknown God." His words should be inscribed somewhere in every church sanctuary. Pointing out that God did not just create the universe but gave to all humans a common ancestor, making us all of one blood, Paul says God's plan was that humans might search for and find God,

> ...though indeed God is not far from each one of us. For in God we live, and move and have our being; as even some of your own poets have said, "For we too are God's offspring."
>
> (paraphrased for inclusive language)

We'll return to Paul's words in Athens in Chapter 14. But you have enough here to get a grounding for a fresh start and some renewed energy for the thrust and grind of living. The acts of the Spirit working in us and through us can still change our world, and us.

PAUL'S WRITINGS

On God's love for us

Speaking of hardships, distresses, and every other dire thing that can happen to us in life, Paul boldly says,

…in all these things we are more than conquerors through him who loved us. For I am convinced that neither death, nor life, nor angels, nor rulers, nor things present, nor things to come, nor powers, nor height, nor depth, nor anything else in all creation, will be able to separate us from the love of God in Christ Jesus our Lord.

Romans 8:37–39

Our response to God's love

I appeal to you…by the mercies of God, to present your bodies as a living sacrifice, holy and acceptable to God, which is your spiritual worship. Do not be conformed to this world [pushed into its mold or values], but be transformed by the renewing of your minds, so that you may discern what is the will of God – what is good and acceptable and perfect.

Romans 12:1–2

The Greek text says literally, "be metamorphosed," as in a caterpillar becoming a butterfly.

A hymn to love

Paul says, in part:

Love is patient; love is kind; love is not envious or boastful or arrogant or rude. It does not insist on its own way; it is not irritable or resentful; it does not rejoice in wrongdoing, but rejoices in the truth. It bears all things, believes all things, hopes all things, endures all things. Love never ends…

1 Corinthians 13:4–8a

Since Paul's great hymn to love in 1 Corinthians 13 is not only the most insightful and eloquent utterance he ever made and thus, rightly, is familiar to almost everyone, there is no need to reproduce it *in toto* here. But it's important to realize that in its fullness it has enormous relevancy for the topic we're addressing. I once wrote a column about "the expulsive power of a new emotion." The idea was not mine originally, but I know from experience that it works. When one is beset by negative thoughts, feelings, and a negative outlook, trying to attack them frontally, head-on, can be a mistake. It only focuses our energy more solidly on them and can, in fact, end up reinforcing them. But if a fresh emotion such as anger – or, much more positively, love – enters into us, it has great power, unconsciously, to throw the negativity out. It expels it and an entirely fresh viewpoint takes its place. Never underestimate the "expulsive power" of a new emotion!

That's why I recommend reading and re-reading all 13 verses of chapter 13. One of the worst parts of feeling overcome by stress is the accompanying sense of being shut in on oneself that so often goes with it. Filling one's mind and heart with words and thoughts about love, and then finding ways in which to express it, however simply, can work wonders. Others are made happy. The obsession with self erodes away.[5]

What time is it?

All the books on meditation, all the world's writings on inner serenity and happiness, insist that the only *real* time we have is *this* day, *this* hour, *this* moment. Even this moment is moving into the past to make way for the next. The time for living in the moment is *now*. Bible time is *now*. Wisdom time is *now*. The spiritual call is always to awaken from the cultural trance we walk in and to do it now:

...you know what time it is, how it is now the moment for you
to wake from sleep. For salvation [wholeness] is nearer to us now
than when we became believers; the night is far gone, the day is near.
Let us then lay aside the works of darkness,
and put on the armor of light; let us live honorably as in the day...
Romans 13:11–13

On not giving in to discouragement

In a culture that values looks, appearance, youthfulness, and all that goes with superficial, external (and hence fleeting) values, many grow discouraged at the advances of age and especially as various stresses leave their visible marks – wrinkles, loss of hair, hearing or eyesight failure, or whatever.

Here's an uplifting mantra-like passage with an entirely different perspective – a spiritual one:

So we do not lose heart. Even though our outer nature [the physical
body] is wasting away [ouch!], our inner nature is being renewed day
by day. For this slight momentary affliction is preparing us for an
eternal weight of glory beyond all measure, because we look not at
what can be seen but at what cannot be seen; for what can be seen is
temporary, but what cannot be seen is eternal.
2 Corinthians 4:16–18

Temples of God

For we are the temple of the living God; as God said,

I will live in them and walk among them,
and I will be their God,
and they shall be my people.

As Paul says elsewhere,

We have this [or hold this] treasure in earthen vessels

– clay pots [in other words, our bodies].
2 Corinthians 6:16

Saints suffer too

Just in case anyone thinks or believes that saints, apostles, gurus, or other holy leaders live lives free from stress, you should read 2 Corinthians 11:16 – 12:10. Here Paul lists his own stresses, weaknesses, and sufferings for all to see. Note his comment that besides all else,

I am under daily pressure [stress] because of my anxiety for all the [young] churches. Who is weak and I am not weak?
2 Corinthians 11:28–29

For a modern parallel one could cite the previously mentioned prayer diary of Mother Teresa, who is currently being fast-tracked for Beatification, the first step in becoming an official Saint of the Roman Catholic Church. Speaking frequently through its pages about her experience of the "absence" of God, she once wrote, "I feel just the terrible pain of God not wanting me, of God not being God, of God not really existing."

Yet out of this weak, troubled, frail person, came virtual miracles and a great, still-ongoing work for humanity and for God. She proved true the seemingly paradoxical words of Paul, when he tells how he had a lifelong "thorn in the flesh." In 2 Corinthians 12:9, Paul writes that God answered his prayer for relief from his problem with these words:

My grace is sufficient for you, for power [or, as in the KJV, my strength] is made perfect in weakness.

The fruit of the Spirit

Living a life that is spiritual is necessarily the opposite of a life lived according to what Paul calls "the flesh" – life at a purely appetite level, the life of grasping attachment to material things and to the physical alone. In Galatians 5:16–26, Paul gives a long list of the "fruits" of such a misguided path, including sexual licentiousness, strife, jealousy, anger, quarreling, envy, and drunkenness. Here's what the apostle has to say about the marks or the products of the spiritual way:

> By contrast, the fruit of the Spirit is love, joy, peace, patience
> [endurance], kindness, generosity, faithfulness, gentleness,
> and self-control.[6]
>
> Galatians 5:22–23

The whole armor of God

For Christians particularly, but for all interested parties as well, Paul's famous description of the spiritual life as a war against evil requiring God's full protection on every side – the famous passage about God's armor – is an essential read. It's a powerful metaphor for those trying to be "spiritual warriors" in our day.

> Finally, be strong in the Lord [God] and in the strength of [God's]
> power. Put on the whole armor of God, so that you may be able to
> stand against the wiles of the devil [forces of evil]. For our struggle is
> not against enemies of blood and flesh, but against…the spiritual
> forces of evil in the heavenly places. Therefore take up the whole armor
> of God, so that you may be able to withstand on that evil day, and
> having done everything, to stand firm. Stand therefore, and fasten the
> belt of truth around your waist, and put on the breastplate of
> righteousness. As shoes for your feet put on whatever will make you
> ready to proclaim the gospel of peace. With all these, take the shield of
> faith…Take the helmet of salvation, and the sword of the Spirit,
> which is the word of God.
> Pray in the Spirit at all times in every prayer and supplication…
>
> Ephesians 6:10–18

We are what we think

Before action, there is thought. As we think, so we are, the Bible says. In other words, thoughts have an enormous power to shape our lives and to help determine whether we are contented, productive, loving people, or the very opposite. However, while we as a culture spend billions of dollars and untold hours of our time upon physical and emotional health, we are often careless about what we allow ourselves to think.

Here's a guide for a spiritually oriented workout for the mind. It comes from Paul's letter to the Philippians.

Finally, beloved, whatever is true, whatever is honorable,
whatever is just, whatever is pure, whatever is pleasing,
whatever is commendable, if there is any excellence and if there is
anything worthy of praise, think about these things.
Keep on doing the things that you have learned and seen in me,
and the God of peace will be with you.

Philippians 4:8–9 (KJV)

SOME BRIEF MEDITATIONS
FROM THE REST OF THE NEW TESTAMENT

God is light and in him is no darkness at all.

1 John 1:5

Let us love one another, because love is from God; everyone who
loves is born of God and knows God.

1 John 4:7

Those who say, "I love God," and hate their brothers or sisters,
are liars; for those who do not love a brother or a sister whom they
have seen, cannot love God whom they have not seen.

1 John 4:20

A final vision of the new Jerusalem

The last two chapters of the New Testament and thus of the Christian Bible, are filled with symbolism, as indeed is the entire Book of Revelation. In a way, their vision may not seem quite to belong here, and yet I intuit that it does. Revelation chapter 21 begins with these moving words:

Then I saw a new heaven and a new earth; for the first heaven and
the first earth had passed away, and the sea was no more. And I saw
the holy city, the new Jerusalem, coming down out of heaven from
God, prepared as a bride adorned for her husband.
And I heard a loud voice from the throne saying,
"See, the home of God is among mortals.
God will dwell with them as their God;
they will be God's peoples,
and God will be with them;
God will wipe every tear from their eyes.
Death will be no more;
mourning and crying and pain will be no more,
for the first things have passed away."
And the one who was seated on the throne said,
"See, I am making all things new."
Revelation 21:1–6 (paraphrased for inclusive language)

A couple of verses further on, God says,

To the thirsty I will give water as a gift
from the spring of the water of life.

The "river of life"

Lastly, in deep symbolism that has always somehow resonated in my depths, the River of Life is gloriously described:

Then the angel showed me the river of the water of life, bright as crystal, flowing from the throne of God and of the Lamb through the middle of the street of the city. On either side of the river, is the tree of life with its twelve kinds of fruit, producing its fruit each month; and the leaves of the tree are for the healing of the nations. Nothing accursed will be found there anymore. But the throne of God and of the Lamb will be in it, and his servants will worship him; they will see his face, and his name will be on their foreheads. And there will be no more night; they need no light of lamp or sun, for the Lord God will be their light and they will reign forever and ever.

Revelation 22:1–5

X

FROM
OTHER FAITHS

BUDDHISM

Buddhists believe that all beings possess Buddha-nature.
In our true nature we are all Buddhas. However, the face of our
Buddha-nature is obscured by karma (the law of causation)
and its traces, which are rooted in grasping at self,
just as the sun is covered by clouds. All beings are the same and
are one in being perfect in their true nature.

Tulku Thondup, *The Healing Power of Mind*[1]

According to Buddhist teaching, our natural, Buddha-nature is always there, the mind is always peaceful in its true being, wisdom is sound and whole. The problem is to get rid of all that clouds or defiles our true self. The method is through meditation and lovingkindness in every act.

For self-examination
And what then are the defilements of the heart? Greed and covetousness, malevolence, anger malice, hypocrisy, spite, envy,

stinginess, deceit, treachery, obstinacy, empty-headed excitement, arrogance, pride, conceit, indolence. If a man thinks and knows that these are defilements of the heart, and strives to get rid of them, he becomes confident in the Buddha.[2]

The goal

The purpose of the Holy Life does not consist in acquiring support, honor or fame, nor in gaining virtue, concentration, or the eye of knowledge. But that unshakeable deliverance of the heart – that indeed is the object of the holy life: that is its essence, that is its goal (OBP, #923, p. 303).

A Buddhist litany for peace

(For use by two or more persons)

As we are together, praying for Peace,
let us truly be with each other.
(Silence)
Let us pay attention to our breathing.
(Silence)
Let us be relaxed in our bodies and our minds.
(Silence)
Let us be at peace with our bodies and minds.
(Silence)
Let us return to ourselves and become wholly ourselves.
Let us maintain a half-smile on our faces.
(Silence)
Let us be aware of the source of being
common to us all and to all living things.
(Silence)
Evoking the sense of the Great Compassion,
let us fill our hearts with our own compassion
– towards ourselves and towards all living beings.
(Silence)

Let us pray that all living beings realize that they are
all brothers and sisters, all nourished from the same source of life.
(Silence)
Let us pray that we ourselves cease to be the cause of
suffering to each other.
(Silence)
Let us plead with ourselves to live in a way which will not deprive
other living beings of air, water, food, shelter, or the chance to live.
(Silence)
With humility, with awareness of the existence of life, and of
the sufferings that are going on around us,
let us pray for the establishment of peace in our hearts and on earth.
Amen.

OBP, pp. 35, 306–307

Buddhist mantras and prayers

The Truthfinder [the Buddha] has proclaimed that
all dangers and fears, and the innumerable sufferings [of life]
arise only from the mind.

OBP, p. 310, #946

Seek, therefore, thine own Wisdom within thee; It is the vast deep.

OBP, p. 311, #949

Have mercy on me, O Beneficent One. I was angered for
I had no shoes: Then I met a man who had no feet.

OBP, p. 313, #954

May I be in peace and let go of my expectations.[3]

For caregivers

May I offer my care and presence unconditionally, knowing they may be met by gratitude, indifference, anger, or anguish.[4]

The classic Buddhist mantra

Om Mani Padma Hum – (Hail to the Jewel in the Lotus)

According to Buddhist priest Roshi Joan Halifax, founder of a Buddhist study center, Upaya, in Santa Fe, New Mexico, these words refer to "the mind of compassion and the mind of clarity in unison with each other."[5]

Confess your hidden faults.
Approach what you find repulsive.
Help those you think you cannot help.
Anything you are attached to, let it go.
Go to the places that scare you.[6]

On loving your enemies – The parable of the saw

The Blessed One said, "Though robbers or high-waymen might carve you limb from limb with a double-handed saw, yet even then whoever gives way to hatred is not a follower of my teaching. You should train yourselves like this: 'Our minds will not become deranged, we will not utter evil speech, we will remain with a friendly heart, devoid of hatred: and, beginning with these people, we will develop the thought of lovingkindness.'"

A prayer for lovingkindness

May I (we, they) be filled with lovingkindness.
May I (we, they) be well.
May I (we, they) be peaceful and at ease.
May I (we, they) be happy.

Source unknown

HINDUISM

Until you have found God in your own soul,
the whole world will seem meaningless to you.

Hinduism

"In the beginning was the Word," says the gospel according to St. John, "and the Word was with God and the Word was God."

This statement echoes, almost exactly, a verse from the Rik Veda:

In the beginning was Brahman (God), with whom was the Word;
and the Word was truly the supreme Brahman.[1]

Hinduism's basic chant or mantra, or, how to retrain your mind

The word which expresses him (Brahman or God) is OM, or AUM, as it is properly pronounced. This word OM should be repeated with meditation upon its meaning, according to Patanjali (Patanjali, #27, #28, p. 56).

Patanjali, the best-known Hindu teacher and editor (c. 400–300 BCE), and the other great Hindu sages realized that our minds of themselves tend to jump about from one topic to feelings, then to other topics in a constant stream. Our moods

168 ~ FINDING THE STILL POINT

then follow these thoughts. "The sun comes out, our mood brightens. Insects begin to buzz around us, and we turn irritable, and nervous. Often it is just as simple as that" (Patanjali, #29, p. 59).

But, he says, if we bring into our inner reveries the repetition of the name of God, "we shall find that we can control our moods, despite interference from the outside world." We are always, anyhow, repeating words in our minds – the name of a friend or enemy, the name of an anxiety, the name of a desired object – and each of these words is surrounded by its own mental climate.

Patanjali suggests a simple test. He says to try saying "war," or "cancer," or "money" ten thousand times, "and you will find that your whole mood has been changed and colored by the associations connected with that word. Similarly, the name of God will change the climate of your mind. It cannot do otherwise" (Patanjali, #29, pp. 59–60).

Emergency measures

When you read the Hindu scriptures, the phrase, "To take refuge in his [God's] name," frequently appears. The Hindu master points out that this same phenomenon occurs many times, too many to be counted, and not just in Hinduism. For example, "They that know thy name will put their trust in thee…" from Psalm 9:10 (KJV). Or in Proverbs 18:10: "The name of the Lord is a strong tower; the righteous run into it and are safe." This may seem merely poetic or, perhaps, even irrelevant to us today. The opposite is true. Patanjali explains that such repetition has great healing power:

When the mind is so violently disturbed by pain or fear
that it cannot be used for meditation or even rational thought,
there is still one thing that you can always do: you can repeat his
name over and over. You can hold fast to that through all the tumult.

Patanjali, #29, p. 60

Hindu wisdom sayings and prayers

KATHA

Om...
May Brahman protect us,
May he guide us,
May he give us strength and right understanding.
May love and harmony be with us all.
Om... Peace – peace – peace.[8]

ISHA

Filled with Brahman are the things we see,
Filled with Brahman are the things we see not,
From out of Brahman floweth all that is:
From Brahman all – yet he is still the same...
Om... Peace – peace – peace.

Upanishads, p. 27

KENA

May quietness descend upon my limbs,
My speech, my breath, my eyes, my ears;
May all my senses wax clear and strong.
May Brahman show himself unto me.
Never may I deny Brahman, nor Brahman me.
I with him and he with me – may we abide always together.
May there be revealed to me,
Who am devoted to Brahman,
The holy truth of the Upanishads.
Om... Peace – peace – peace.

Upanishads, p. 30

PRASNA

With our ears may we hear what is good.
With our eyes may we behold thy righteousness.
Tranquil in body, may we who worship thee find rest.
OM... Peace – peace – peace.
OM... Hail to the supreme Self!

Upanishads, p. 35

A breathing mantra

The mind may also be calmed by expulsion and retention of the breath (Patanjali, #34). Patanjali's translators observe,

> *First, we must note that Patanjali sees control of the mind as a psychophysical problem. In this he agrees with modern scientific thought. Studies of breathing have shown that the method of respiration affects the whole organism. Calmness can actually be introduced by deep, steady inhalations and exhalations.* Mental disturbance and despondency are accompanied by irregular breathing; rapid, shallow and uncontrolled

Patanjali, p. 68–69 (emphasis mine)

The "Inner Light"

Thou are That.

Hinduism's Core Belief

The goal or aim of Hinduism is to know one's union with Brahman. It can be put another way; union with Brahman comes through union with the Atman (the Divine Presence) within.

Patanjali says, in instruction 36, "Concentration may also be attained by fixing the mind upon the Inner Light, which is beyond sorrow."

His commentary says:

The ancient yogis believed there was an actual center of spiritual consciousness called "The Lotus of the Heart," situated between the abdomen and the thorax, which could be revealed in deep meditation. They claimed that it had the form of a lotus (flower) and that it shone with an inner light. It was said to be "beyond sorrow," since those who saw it were filled with an extraordinary sense of peace and joy.

Patanjali, p. 71

In the Chandogya Upanishad, one can read how the light, lotus, or "little house in the heart," is where God (Brahman) dwells. There's more:

Even so large as the universe outside is the universe within the lotus of the heart. Within it are heaven and earth, the sun, the moon, the lightning and all the stars. Whatever is in the macrocosm is in the microcosm also.

Patanjali, p. 72

Summing up

The full resources of genuine yoga and Hinduism in general for responding to stress are virtually unlimited. What's more, they can be used with integrity by people of all faiths or none. We conclude this brief treatment with a famous poem by a great Hindu saint, Kabir:

I laugh when I hear that the fish in the water is thirsty.
You wander restlessly from forest to forest while the Reality
is within your own dwelling.
The truth is here! Go where you will – until you have found God
in your own soul, the whole world will seem meaningless to you.

Patanjali, p. 77

In late November and early December, 2001, the Beatles were suddenly in everyone's mind. There was the 21st anniversary of the murder of John Lennon and the overshadowing event of George Harrison's death from cancer. Harrison, as is well-known, had become a devout Hindu and the world was deeply touched by the tribute of his wife, Olivia, and son Dhani: "The profound beauty of the moment of George's passing – of his awakening from this dream – was no surprise to those of us who knew how he longed to be with God. In that pursuit, he was relentless."[9]

ISLAM

O Lord, grant us to love Thee:
grant that we may love those that love Thee;
grant that we may do the deeds that win Thy love.

Muhammad, 7th century CE[10]

In spite of its many historical and artistic achievements, and its great spiritual power, not to mention its growing membership of just over one billion followers, the religion of Islam has not yet been well understood in the Western world. Thankfully, one of the more positive results of the "War on Terrorism" and the events that spawned it has been that the Muslim faith has received a higher profile and much better treatment in the media. But in far too many minds it is still synonymous with violence, fanaticism, and terrorism. This is a great tragedy, because true Islam adheres to and follows the very same moral and spiritual values that prevail in Judaism, Christianity, and the rest of the other major religions. ("Islam" means submission to God or Allah.)

In truth, Islam, Judaism, and Christianity have much more in common than things that divide them. They all claim Abraham as their father. They share all the prophets and other Old Testament characters: Noah, Moses, Joseph, Isaac, Ishmael, and Jacob or "Israel." Jesus is a great prophet according to Muslim teaching.

When once I wrote a Sunday column expressing doubts about a literal understanding of the Virgin Birth, I got more letters of protest from devout Muslims than from Christians! Islam values peace as much or more than other faiths and is opposed to war except in self-defense. The term *jihad*, which so often is associated – by the West and by fanatical fringes in Islam – with a so-called "holy war" against the U.S. in particular and the West in general, means simply to struggle or work for the faith and its preservation.

But you don't have to take my word for any of this. In the admittedly brief selection of verses from the Qur'an and prayers or mantras from other Muslim sources, non-Muslim readers can test the "product" for themselves. The all-encompassing faith, obedience, and submission to God (Allah) taught and demanded by Islam, together with the simple yet highly formative practice of daily prayers (five times a day, facing in the direction of Mecca, in Saudi Arabia) and other explicit duties, give followers a deep sense of security. They believe deeply that, ultimately, nothing can happen that is outside God's will. They are exposed to the same assaults from stress that we all are. Yet overall, it has been my lifetime's observation that their faith, well-practiced, is re-markably suited to help them adapt to and respond in a healthy way to the anxieties of modern living.

Some resources from the Qur'an

In the Name of God, the merciful Lord of mercy.
Praise be to God, the Lord of all being,
the merciful Lord of mercy,
Master of the day of judgement.
You alone we serve: to You alone we come for aid.

Guide us in the straight path.
the path of those whom You have blessed,
not of those against whom there is displeasure,
nor of those who go astray.[11]

O my Lord, let security and truth precede and follow me wherever
You lead me. Let authority and succour from
Your presence be with me.
OBP, Sura 17:80

He (Noah) called upon his Lord, saying:
"Things overwhelm me: come to my help."
OBP, Sura 54:10

Note: In this case, the mantra or repeated assertion would be

Lord, things overwhelm me: come to my help.

Our Lord, give us mercy from Your presence and let a right wisdom
order the situation in which we find ourselves.
OBP, Sura 18:10

Our Lord, we have believed. Forgive us and have mercy on us.
Yours is the utmost mercy.
OBP, Sura 23:109

And when My servants ask thee about Me, say: "I am near.
I answer the prayer of the supplicant when he prays to Me.
So they should harken to Me and believe in Me,
that they may follow the right way."[12]

Allah is the friend of those who believe: He brings them out of every
kind of darkness into light...
HQ, Sura 2:258

Our Lord, burden us not with what we have not the strength to bear;
and efface our sins, and grant us forgiveness and have mercy on us;
Thou are our master...

HQ, Sura 2:287

If Allah help you, none shall overcome you; but if He forsake you,
then who is there that can help you beside Him?
In Allah, then, let the believers put their trust.

HQ, Sura 3:161

And ask forgiveness of Allah. Surely, Allah is
Most Forgiving, Merciful.

HQ, Sura 4:107

And to Allah belongs all that is in the heavens and all that is in the
earth; and Allah encompasses all things.

HQ, Sura 4:127

There has come to you indeed from Allah a Light, and a clear Book.
Thereby does Allah guide those who seek His pleasure on the paths of
peace, and leads them out of every kind of darkness into light by His
will, and guides them to the right path.

HQ, Sura 16b–17:5

And He it is Who created the heavens and the earth in accordance
with the requirements of wisdom; and the day he says "Be!" it will
be. His word is the truth and His will be the Kingdom on the day
when the trumpet will be blown. He is the Knower of the unseen and
the seen. And He is the Wise, the All-Aware.

HQ, Sura 6:74

He causes the break of day; and He made the night for rest and
the sun and the moon for reckoning time.
That is the decree of the Mighty, the Wise. And He it is Who has
made the stars for you that you may follow the right direction with
their help amid the deep darkness of the land and the sea...
HQ, Sura 6:97–98

Surely, this Qur'an guides to what is most right; and gives to
the believers who do good deeds the glad tidings
that they shall have a great reward.
HQ, Sura 17:10

Verily, those who say, "Our Lord is Allah," and then remain steadfast
– no fear shall come upon them, nor shall they grieve.
HQ, Sura 46:14

And he who submits himself completely to Allah, and is a doer of
good, he has surely grasped a strong handle.
And with Allah rests the end of all affairs
HQ, Sura 31:23

Who has made perfect everything He has created.
And he began the creation of man from clay. Then He made his
progeny from an extract of an insignificant fluid. Then he fashioned
him and breathed into him of His spirit...
HQ, Sura 32: 8, 9, 10

So, have patience. Surely the promises of Allah are true.
And ask forgiveness for thy frailty, and glorify thy Lord with
His praise in the evening and in the morning.
HQ, Sura 40:56

He is the living God. There is no God but He.
So pray unto Him, being sincere to Him in religion.
All praise belongs to Allah, the Lord of the worlds.

HQ, Sura 40:66

And I said, "Seek forgiveness of your Lord;
for He is the Great Forgiver."

HQ, Sura 71:11

And they [the virtuous] feed, for love of Him, the poor, the orphan,
and the prisoner, Saying, "We feed you for Allah's pleasure only.
We desire no reward nor thanks from you."

HQ, Sura 76: 9, 10

O my God, I am not the first to transgress and find Your pardon nor
to resist Your good purpose and yet to experience Your gracious dealing.
'Tis You who responds to the cry of the distressful, unveiling the
source of their distress, knowing every secret thing.
Great is Your righteousness.

OBP, p. 334

A prayer ascribed to Muhammad:

O God give me light in my heart and light in my tongue,
and light in my hearing and light in my sight, and light in
my feeling and light in all my body, and light before me
and light behind me. Give me, I pray Thee, light on my
right hand and light on my left hand and light above me
and light beneath me; O Lord, increase light within me
and give me light, and illumine me.

OBP, p. 343

As is fitting, I want to end this small sample of various expressions of Muslim spirituality with a "closing Muslim Prayer":

> *O Lord, may the end of my life be the best of it;*
> *may my closing acts be my best acts,*
> *and may the best of my days be the day when I shall meet Thee.*
> OBP, p. 344

Now it's time to turn to the more theological part of this book – what Jesus discovered and how religions in general, and Christianity in particular, can meet some of the challenges of this new but already sullied millennium.

PART FOUR

THE
GOD
WITHIN

XI

PROLOGUE AND CREEDS

There is something that can be found in one place. It is a great treasure, which may be called the fulfillment of existence. The place where this treasure can be found is the place on which one stands.

Most of us achieve only at rare moments a clear realization of the fact that we have never tasted the fulfillment of existence, that our lives do not participate in true, fulfilled existence, that, as it were, it passes true existence by. We nevertheless feel the deficiency at every moment, and in some measure strive to find — somewhere — what we are seeking. Somewhere, in some province of the world or of the mind, except where we stand, where we have been set — but it is there and nowhere else that the treasure can be found. The environment which I feel to be the natural one, the situation which has been assigned to me as my fate, the things that happen to me day after day, the things that claim me day after day — these contain my essential task and such fulfillment of existence as is open to me. It is said of a certain Talmudic master that the paths of Heaven

were as bright to him as the streets of a man's native town.
It is a greater thing if the streets of a man's native town are
as bright to him as the paths of Heaven. For it is here,
where we stand, that we should try to make shine the light
of the hidden divine life.

Martin Buber, *The Way of Man*[1]

PROLOGUE

Growing up as a boy from a working class, Irish immigrant family in the east end of Toronto, I spent most of my early, non-school time playing in the narrow streets and the network of lanes behind the houses. These were the years of the Great Depression, which began a few months after my birth, and then of World War II which broke out a decade later. One of our favorite pastimes as youngsters, following hard upon an obsession with playing "Cowboys and Indians," was playing "alleys," or shooting marbles. There was every conceivable variation of theme: trying to see how many one could toss into a small hollow scraped in the ground about three paces away; how close to a specific wall one could roll the brightly colored glass or stone globes; who could win the most marbles by taking turns trying to hit the other person's large "glassy" or "agate." Each hit won one marble. At the end of the day, each of us would roll out the contents of his "marble bag" – my mum had made me one out of some leftover cloth from her home sewing, complete with drawstring – and examine the contents. It mattered a lot what the number, size, and beauty of the alleys added up to. It was an important stock-taking. A moment of truth and of reflection upon it.

This book is like that. I have recently reached a significant date in my life. Thankfully, I have seldom felt more well and energized and happy. But it's a fitting, biblical time, three score years plus ten, to reflect on and examine any "jewels" found on life's path thus far. I'm eager to share what has done more for my spiritual life and understanding than anything else over years of study, reflection, and an amazingly varied experience of life. It has to do with crucial, existential matters such as the true self-identity of each of us, our chief purpose in life, and the very core nature of the Christian message, indeed of all true religion.

The Bible's first creation account, as we have seen, tells us that God made humankind (Adam) in God's own image. This *Imago Dei*, as it is called – the image of God – has been the occasion of a lot of commentary and controversy down the ages. The early Church Fathers saw in it a reference to our possession of free-will, a reference to our supposed superiority to all other creatures, our alleged possession of immortality, or our gift of self-reflective reason. In the more mystical tradition of the churches both of East and West, however, the concept of the Imago Dei has played a crucial role as the point at which the soul is *capax Dei*, capable of knowing God and hence of entering into ultimate union with God. Not ultimate absorption as in some forms of Buddhism and Hinduism, but union.

I say this in total awareness of the way in which both Roman Catholic and Protestant theology since their earliest days have choked out this kind of "high view" of humanity in favor of a much gloomier, more dour estimate of our nature and proclivities. Obsessed with the notion of the "Fall" in the great myth of the Garden of Eden and its purported flawing of the Imago, many great Western theologians have emphasized almost gleefully the depravity and corruption brought by sin – for example, St. Augustine, Jerome and Tertullian in the first centuries CE, and Karl Barth and Emil Brunner much more recently. Indeed, Barth held that because of sin, humanity is totally incapable of any knowledge of God apart from revelation, that is, Holy Writ. Centuries of teaching only this view of the human has brought nothing but incredible misery and spiritual inertia, I now believe.

The proof is out there for all to see. In the United States, for example, a major mental health issue is that untold millions seem incapable of holding a reasonable sense of self-worth and self-esteem. This, in spite of the prevailing religiosity – chiefly ultra-conservative evangelicalism, plus the "civil religion" espoused by most U.S. presidents – which insists its message is one of abundant life and of unfettered affirmation of the supreme value of each and every "sinner" out there. But first, of course, as watching any evangelistic "crusade" on television will prove, the person who is to inherit all this "abundant life" has to be roasted over the fires of a literal hell and be fully assured of how unworthy he or she really is of God's grace. The overwhelming spate of self-help books, tapes, and videos now flooding the bookstores in North America is but a small symptom of what is truly a pandemic disorder, the negative results of a negative theology.

I believe the profound, biblical concept of our having been created "in the image of God," goes even deeper than some of the early Fathers and many of the more humane scholars in the past have said. To be made in the Imago Dei is to share now, in some way in this world, in the nature and essence of God. It is not just a capacity or a remote potentiality, but an inner reality. We have each been given "something of God" within us. To cite the opening verses of John's gospel, the Logos, which was in the beginning both present with God and belonging to the essence of God, was the "true Light" which gives its/his light to every human being who "comes into the world."

The vast majority of Bible scholars today agree that John's opening verses, The Prologue, consciously and deliberately echo the opening words of Genesis in order to show that a fresh start is being made. Thus, the references to the Imago Dei, in Genesis, and the statement that the divine light is bequeathed to every human being at birth, in the Gospel of John, are linked tightly together. Both assert the presence of the divine Spirit or an individuated "portion" of God in the human heart. This latter is a metaphorical manner of speaking, of course. God cannot be divided up.

Let me say it again. What this means in bold terms is that we are all, regardless of creed, color, or culture, children of God – "sons and daughters of God" – and as such, bearers of God's own divine life within. This, as we have seen, is not some New Age, simplistic wishing, but the clear witness of the entire Bible, particularly of the New Testament, once the reader divests himself/herself from years of cover-up and/or distortion from traditional church preaching and teaching. I call this proclamation of the essential divinity of every human, Core Christianity. Though externally it might seem quite different from Eastern and other religions, Core Christianity is very much like them after all – a specific form of the Perennial Philosophy which is embodied in every faith.

According to the Perennial Philosophy, the whole purpose of life is to find out who you really are – the offspring of God, bearing God within as your higher self – and to see what your purpose is; to become awakened to this knowledge and to let this Light shine through you for fulfilling your own potential and that of all others in community, until a much fuller, eternal union dawns upon a "distant shore." Years of study and experience have long convinced me that basic Christianity is about this "Christ Principle" or "Christ Consciousness," as some prefer to call it, which Jesus discovered himself and which he proclaimed as Good News or gospel for all prepared to receive it. In what follows, we'll trace out in greater detail the origins and nature of this message and examine its implications for churched and non-churched alike.

THE BACKGROUND

I say, "You are gods, children of the Most High,
all of you."
Psalm 82:6

Is it not written in your law, "I said, you are gods"?
Jesus Christ (John 10:34)

In the introduction, it was stated that Christianity today is in the grip of a crisis of monumental proportions. Nothing that has happened in the previous 2,000 years of church history has come close to the present convulsion and increasing chaos that is shaking the church's deepest foundations, a predicament that will almost certainly only worsen to the point of threatening the very existence of the hundreds of kinds of churches around the globe. The future – if you project on a graph the current decline of the church in Europe and in North America – looks worse than bleak.

Many, both inside and outside the fold, are now articulating this ominous prophecy. John Spong, recently retired bishop of Newark, New Jersey, and the most high-profile of all the doomsters, has titled one of his latest volumes *Why Christianity Must Change or Die.* In 12 theses, a la Martin Luther, only this time not nailed to a church door but trumpeted first in his book and on the Internet, Spong makes clear that he's not talking about superficial cosmetic changes or about minor adjustments to sundry quaint aspects of faith and order. What the bishop's theses state quite bluntly is that the changes required will necessitate a completely radical transformation of the content of the historic creeds. It's no longer a matter of simply trying to update the church's language, but of transforming the conceptual framework and the inner essence of what is believed and promulgated. The urgent need is to make the foundations of faith square honestly with modern thinking – especially when it comes to reconciling faith with science and the comparatively recent discoveries in psychology, biology, physics, and cosmology.

But in reading Spong and the others who seem to be saying "The church is dead" rather than "God is dead," as some theologians loudly argued in the mid-1960s, one can come away wondering why, when most of their points are so reasonable and seemingly so inevitable, this entire trend leaves the seeker-after-truth still feeling so strangely empty. At least to date, they hand on such meager leftovers after all their probings that any idea of the churches having some "Good News" to impart, or of fulfilling a mission of bringing peace and wholeness to the world, seems to vanish. Spong, for example, argues persuasively that a theistic God who is "out there" – a sort of heavenly Superman – ready to intervene in the world arbitrarily if we pray hard enough, no longer makes any sense. I agree. But, so far, he has done very little to even "sketch in" what his non-theistic God is or does. Certainly what is not needed or wanted is a cool, indifferent God essence or spirit who, on further thought, can best be described in abstract terms denoting something very like a cosmic ether, a vague force, or an impassive energy field. Spong's latest book is *A New Christianity for a New World*. His ideas of God may satisfy him, but they are unlikely to speak to many others. This is not the "God of the Gaps" for certain. This God is a gap itself!

The question, then, is, can one find anything fully solid to cling to, given the vortex of Spongian-type attacks upon the theological status quo, mixed with the sceptical assessments by theologians, such as the Jesus Seminar's New Testament scholars, of the role of Jesus in the formation of the gospels? What, in the light of our questing, is the deepest message of the scriptures, both the Hebrew Bible and the canonical New Testament writings, particularly the four gospels? Has such a message got any timely, life-changing implications for modern young people and adults as well? Can this message not just make a leap into the place once taken by the traditional obsessions with sin, punishment, salvation, and saintliness, but also wholly inspire members and non-members alike with a fresh vision of what Christianity – and all the other major religious faiths for that matter – truly embodies?

This is the issue before us in this part of our investigation. To anticipate, the key thesis which will shortly emerge more clearly is that there is indeed a different way of looking at the earliest documents and at the teaching of Jesus as it is traced in them. There is an aspect, a deep, underlying theme of all his offhand sayings, his parables and sermons – and, of course, of his life as lived – that has not received sufficient attention in Western Christianity. Too much ink (and blood as well) has been spilled over the matter of the divinity of Jesus Christ. The time has now come to look more closely at what he and his followers taught about the divinity of humanity, the "godness" of every human being who has ever lived. After thinking, reading, and reflecting on this matter – while teaching at my old seminary, while covering religion around the world as a journalist, between writing other books and regular columns on ethics and spirituality for *The Toronto Star* for the past 30 years – I am even more fully convinced than I was when I wrote *For Christ's Sake* in 1986 that Jesus' chief teaching was not about sin and certainly not about founding a new religion. It was about the kingdom of God, God's active presence everywhere. More specifically, it was about the kingdom as an inner reality – the divinity of every one of us. God in our midst; God within.

To put it another way. What was it that Jesus discovered about himself? Did he feel that this discovery was for himself alone? Or was he referring to that discovery when he said, "The kingdom of heaven is within you?" Or again, when he said, "You shall do greater things than these" (i.e., the works and signs of his ministry)? Or on those occasions when he said to the disciples, "You are the light of the world"? We turn shortly to the evidence that overwhelmingly supports this view. In the end, we will face the crucial question: if Jesus taught the potential divinity of humans, how does that affect the church's thinking and direction for the immediate future and beyond? What does it tell us about a spiritual response to stress?

THE CREEDS

I know that age to age succeeds,
Blowing a noise of tongues and deeds,
A dust of systems and of creeds.
Alfred Lord Tennyson, (1809–1892)[2]

What causes me the most distress as I survey the signs everywhere that this new millennium is destined to be truly "The Spiritual Age," is the feebleness so far of the response of the church and of other faiths to this challenge. In what follows, the major focus is on the Christian church in its numerous manifestations, but not narrowly so. The parallels with other world religions is striking and must not be ignored.

Right now, extremely liberal denominations and their clergy risk being so concerned about communicating with the secularized world – a laudable aim in itself – that they frequently end up becoming a precise copy of it. Many differ little from the local Rotary or Lions Club, apart from their own inexorable passion for ecclesiastical garments and new twists on ancient ceremonies. Liberals are left with little or no Good News to proclaim. Occasionally, to give full credit where it is deserved, they manage to be prophetic on crucial social justice issues. That's good. Most commendable, in fact. But for the millions aching for inner peace and a vital relationship with God, the source of everything, they bring small comfort. They have lost what used to be called "the care of souls." People demand "bread" – in other words, spiritual sustenance, a sense of purpose, a sense of meaning and of their belonging to the cosmos. They are given stones instead. In the attempt to be relevant, many belonging to this wing have fallen into the morass Paul warned about in Romans: "Do not be conformed to this world…" The Greek says literally, "Don't be pressed into this world's mold."

If anything, the state of the ultra-conservatives and that of fundamentalists of every kind is much worse. Taking the overall situation in North America, these groups make up the large majority and seem to be growing. They have great political clout in the United States, particularly. For example, the swift exit of Senator John McCain from the race for the Democratic nomination as presidential candidate for the November 2000 election was due almost entirely to his courage or rashness in attacking the right-wing, "born-again" Republicans who were so keenly engaged in opposing him. Because of their understanding of mass media and its importance in winning the hearts and minds of contemporary seekers, the conservatives almost entirely dominate the field of religion on television. They are behind the publication of an unending flood of books, many of them preoccupied with apocalyptic "facts" about the "End Times." The result is that the prevailing public image or concept of what it means to be a Christian today has been defined in terms of belonging to the "born-again" style of faith. Naturally, those outsiders who are put off by all of the simplistic rigidities tend to identify the whole of faith with this anti-intellectual approach and thus throw out everything – baby, bathwater, and the tub too, so to speak.

The fundamentalists' essential response to the profound intellectual, emotional, and cultural changes of this unique moment, this kairos in history, is to dig in ferociously and keep on repeating the things they have always said. Only they say them much more loudly and insistently than ever before. While there is nothing else today, no field of human thought or endeavor, that has not been forced to make huge, revolutionary shifts in basic concepts, structures, and tactics, religions in general and religious conservatives especially feverishly resist this reality. Using their main weapon, a so-called "infallible" book, the Bible (for which I have enormous love and respect), and interpreting it in their own, literalistic and uncritical way (which is really a 20th-century heresy unknown in earlier times), they preach as their gospel an "old, old story," that now only makes sense if you suspend all rational thought completely.

Critics have spoken out regarding the so-called "dumbing down" of America. It's interesting to study the way in which modern mass media, especially on this continent but by no means only here, have so catered to the lowest common denominator that our culture is indeed becoming shallower and flakier by the day. But so far, nobody I'm aware of has really researched the dumbing-down of Christianity that has gone on at an accelerating pace over the past 60 years or so. As the old millennium finally drew to a close, the growing spiritual hunger of the "unchurched and the "churched" alike was matched step by step with a growing anti-brain, anti-intellectual approach being taken by the conservative stratum in Protestantism and Roman Catholicism alike. These "true-believers" have equated being true to the "faith of our fathers" with simplification, literalism, and black or white answers to any personal or social dilemma, from the so-called "hormone issues," to gun control, to raising a family, to politics in general.

On a recent trip already referred to, Susan and I spent some weeks in northern and central Florida. We spent the time, apart from walking on pristine beaches near Destin and Sandestin, reading, walking, watching the dolphins, and doing research for my writing. Among other things, we deliberately attended a different church each Sunday for several weeks. The first was a charismatic Episcopal church in Destin. Next came a very large Roman Catholic congregation in the same town. These were followed by a Southern Baptist, a Methodist, and an United Presbyterian congregations in the same region. They were all packed, except for the Presbyterian. Every single one we visited was friendly. The people seemed happy and normal. What was extraordinary, however, was the similarity of the sermons. They all came from one mold. You closed your eyes and it could have been the same preacher in every instance. Each homily, apart from the odd illustration or two, could have been preached 75 to 150 years ago. It made no difference that almost everyone there had seen humans walking on the moon, that quantum physics had stood Isaac Newton on his head, that doctors can operate on the heart of a fetus, or transplant whole organs, or that astronomers and astrophysicists assert that there are billions of galaxies in a universe that seems to expand ad infinitum.

In short, the messages were utterly void of any sense of how vastly our thinking and outlook – our worldview – has altered. The concepts, the images, the basic meaning of the Good News being proclaimed were like an alien discourse. The sermons only took on coherence and sense within their own framework and on their own axioms. Your mind, as I've said before, had to be checked at the door, hung on the rack with your coat.

A group of men, including an atheist, a couple of lapsed churchgoers, and several others who are mainly Anglicans but who all find present worship and dogma not only problematic but even a major stumbling block to spiritual growth of any kind, meet once a month in our home. Calling themselves "The Seekers," they tackle head-on the issues raised by trying to remain believers at such a time as this. At a recent session, they each described their increasing inability to recite either the Apostles' or the Nicene Creed with any feeling of integrity. Like millions of others today, they are keen to know and serve God. But the creedal statements, created and gestated in a pre-Copernican world and articulated for the first four or five centuries by theologians and bishops whose worldview and language were those of the Hellenistic world, are simply no longer comprehensible or relevant today. Nor is traditional, orthodox theology in general, which, beginning with the myth of the "Fall" in the

Garden of Eden, is founded upon wholly outdated ideas of Original Sin, Atonement by a wholly pure and innocent sacrifice given by God to "himself," and Salvation through being cleansed and "washed in the blood of the Lamb."

For many years, I have tried strenuously to take each phrase of the Creeds in a symbolic or purely spiritual fashion. I have done so partly out of a vague sense of guilt, partly from a strong desire to identify with the millions of Christians who have gone before us by clinging to the historic formulae or principles for which they often fought and died. At the same time, however, I have felt a deep bond with some words of the late scholar and teacher Bishop Stephen Neill. Neill, a man of honesty and knowledge, said, "There are times when the only part of the creeds that I feel at all sure and comfortable with are those historically based words, 'And was crucified under Pontius Pilate.'" We know of Pontius Pilate from other sources than the Bible. He was a genuine historic figure. I have often quoted Neill on this because I have come to know quite intimately the dilemma he faced.

I can say the opening lines about God creating the heavens and the earth, but once they begin to list such dogmas as the literal Virgin Birth or Jesus' Ascension into heaven "where he sitteth at the right hand of the Father," coherence and credibility come to an end. There are many millions still in the pews for whom this is also true. Many others cannot even get that far! Certainly, many people remain and join heartily in saying the Creeds in spite of their deep-down unbelief. They have made a "tacit deal" to ignore a lot. They know well that the propositions to which they're giving apparent, verbal assent, are built on ancient, untenable beliefs in a three-decker universe and in ideas of the seating protocols of Oriental kings or potentates from 1,900 years ago. Many merely mumble something and ignore the problem of trying to follow the commandment of loving God "with all your mind." Most are in a zombie-like state of consciousness anyway and just let the whole liturgy roll completely over their heads, unexamined and unexplained. Eventually, these people will either wake out of their trance and listen to what they are repeating Sunday by Sunday or drop out in any case because of age, ill-health, or death. When this happens, there is little sign that the next generation will take over and/or continue in the faith once known to our "fathers." The institutional "death" of which Spong and others warn will then be upon us.

The most striking thing about both The Apostle's Creed and The Nicene Creed is what they leave out. For example, they say absolutely nothing about the key teaching of Jesus about the kingdom of God, which includes the entire ethic of social justice – the theme both of Old Testament prophets and of Jesus. This theme of the reign of the kingdom of God, which totally dominates the synoptic gospels – Paul gives it exceedingly short shrift, mentioning it only a few times in contrast to the scores of instances in say, Matthew and Luke – is simply not present in the creeds. The more one thinks about this the more astonishing it becomes. However, other omissions are just as difficult to explain: for example, the Sermon on the Mount's ethic of the Golden Rule, or the vital Jesus-teaching (and, of course, Pauline as well) about the way of love and forgiveness as the hallmark of Christ-like living.

One could go on. But even if you recognize the need to formulate some brief, basic beliefs into creedal-like statements for the sake of brevity and focus, the glaring imbalance of so much emphasis upon ideas Jesus never expressly taught compared with the complete absence of the chief issues which he constantly addressed, screams out that there is something fundamentally wrong.

There is no doubt left in my mind that this is one more powerful reason why the ancient creeds should be retired from active duty and be replaced by others more truly authentic, honest, and clear.

In the novel *The Babes in the Darkling Woods*, by H. G. Wells, one of the puzzled young people in conversation with a country vicar says, "At the back of all, there surely has to be a creed, a fundamental statement, put in language which doesn't conflict with every reality we know about the world. We don't want to be put off with serpents and fig leafs and sacrificial lambs. We want a creed in modern English, sir, and we can't find it."

The following is a slightly updated version of a tentative "creed" that I wrote and published in 1986:

We believe, and put our trust in God, Creator and Sustainer of all things, from the farthest-flung galaxies to the most microscopic forms of life; God is above and around and within everyone of us, and yet so far beyond us in transcendence that our minds cannot fathom the mystery, and our only response is wonder and worship. And we believe God sent Jesus, anointing him in the power of Spirit, to declare by word and deed the gospel of personal and social liberation from the power of fear and all injustice and oppression. Though he was cruelly and unjustly murdered, God raised him from death and God's seal is set forever on Jesus' message and ministry. In him we know that God is love, and that forgiveness and acceptance are ours always. In him we are called to realize God's kingdom in our own lives and in the lives of others. In him we are called to join with God in making all things new. We believe God has granted to us and to all humanity the same Spirit that was in Jesus, creating community and empowering us to be like him. We believe in a dimension of existence yet to come. We seek to build God's kingdom here, but we also look beyond to a day when wars will end and God's New Jerusalem will be revealed. We believe. God help our unbelief.[3]

This "creed" makes no claim whatever to be perfect. No creed will be. But it shows the direction in which I believe we could move. I challenge readers to take the time to create a creed for themselves. Discuss it and improve upon it with others. Simplify!

XII

WHAT JESUS FOUND

God is not a Person living in a particular place outside of the world.
Our search for God is simply a method of finding God inside...
Outside search should remind us that we are forgetting that
God is within us.

Baba Hari Dass, Aphorism 8[1]

I'm aware that readers will differ in their levels of interest and scholarship where interpretation of scripture is at issue. However, the next three chapters, though possibly a challenge, contain the crucial theological underpinnings of the entire book. They represent a fresh approach to understanding what spirituality in general and Christian spirituality in particular are about. Themes already touched upon briefly or simply hinted at in my earlier work are finally melded into a fully developed, consistent, relevant approach – both to stress and, more widely, to the whole of life itself.

THE PUZZLE OF JOHN THE BAPTIST

You don't have to be a biblical scholar to realize, as you read the New Testament, that Jesus' vision and ministry began with his baptism at the hands of John the Baptist in the Jordan. Mark, the earliest gospel, immediately opens its story of "God's good news" with this event. John's gospel describes the baptism in the very first chapter. Matthew and Luke both turn to it as soon as their cycle of traditions about the birth of Jesus have been set out. Without question, the baptism of Jesus was recognized by the earliest Christians as a decisive moment of special illumination, calling, and commitment. It parallels yet far surpasses the call of God to Moses, to Samuel, to Isaiah, and to all the other great prophets of Israel's past.

The less obvious fact, until one's attention is drawn to it, is that while this pivotal story had to be told, it presented some real difficulties for the New Testament authors. In the light of gradually forming ideas about the person of Jesus, the thinkers in the early church were clearly troubled that Jesus had to be baptized at all. As they came to regard him as the "sacrificial lamb without spot or blemish," totally without sin, and since John's baptism was one of repentance and ritual cleansing from sin, they were faced increasingly with an embarrassing theological problem. Why did Jesus have to be baptized? The problem became acute when the task of putting the story down in writing presented itself. If you read all four gospel accounts in succession, ending with that of John, you will quickly see what I mean.

Mark's account (Mark 1:1–9), written about 64–70 CE, some 30 years after the death of Christ, is simple and, apart from having the Baptist make it plain that Jesus is much superior to him – "the latchet of whose shoes I am not worthy to stoop down and unloose" (KJV) – there is no evidence of discomfort that I can discern. Matthew, written some 20 years afterwards, is a different story. When Jesus offers himself for baptism, we are told, "John would have prevented him, saying, 'I need to be baptized by you..."' Jesus replies, "Let it be so now; for it is proper for us in this way to fulfill all righteousness" (Matthew 3:14–15). Only then did John the Baptist give his consent. Notice that the author tries to solve the difficulty by making his baptism the result of Jesus' own command and by interpreting it as a kind of conformist act or outward rite rather than as an admission by Jesus of any real need for repentance and forgiveness.

In Luke's version, roughly contemporary with Matthew's, there is no refusal by John the Baptist or commentary on the reasons for Jesus' submission to the symbolic cleansing. But the superior status of Jesus is left in no doubt whatever. Luke goes beyond both Mark and Matthew in saying that everybody was wondering whether or not John the Baptist was the Christ. It's in that context that Luke has the Baptist repeat his admission that "one mightier than I cometh, the latchet of whose shoes..." (KJV). In other words, the insistence on Jesus' superiority, first given in Mark, is heightened much further.

The latest gospel of all, John – probably written between 90–95 CE – goes to the greatest lengths to counter any possible criticism that the one who baptizes (i.e., John the Baptist) must of necessity be spiritually superior to the one being baptized (i.e., Jesus) or that the fact of the baptism contradicts Jesus' freedom from sin. In this account (John 1:19–32), the Baptist repeatedly has to explain who he is, why he is not the Christ, and who Jesus truly is. He is made to say explicitly that the baptism must happen in order that Jesus "might be revealed to Israel." The actual baptism is not described as in the other three gospels. Instead, John the Baptist says that he himself saw the Spirit descending and remaining on Jesus.

It has been necessary to go into this in some detail to emphasize again just how central the baptism experience of Jesus was to all that was to come after. In a word, the earliest tradition surrounding the baptism and underlining its importance was so strong that the gospel writers had no choice but to include it, in spite of the problems it raised for them and their prospective audiences. They explained away the difficulties as best they could. Significantly, John the Baptist was so highly thought of in the earliest days that groups of his disciples were still together in the period of the nascent church's first missionary outreach, described in Acts.[2]

The baptism itself

Contrary to much popular Christian thinking, whatever momentous experience and insight came to Jesus at the time of his baptism by John, it was first of all an internal, private phenomenon. It was Jesus' own experience. Thus, the source for the written account must have been his own description of it later on to the disciples. Its importance comes from the significance he told them that it had for him. If CNN or some other news agency with modern television cameras and reporters had been there to witness it, they would have captured nothing of the vision in which the heavens were opened and the Holy Spirit descended upon him "like a dove." Nor would they have heard the voice which said, "You are my Son, the Beloved; with you I am well pleased." The first three gospels, the synoptics, do not give the slightest indication that anyone else saw or heard anything out of the ordinary. The fourth gospel would have us believe that it was John the Baptist who saw the dove-like descent of the Spirit: "And John testified, 'I saw the Spirit descending from heaven like a dove, and it remained on him.'" But, as we have already seen, the entire role of the Baptist is expanded and enhanced in this gospel. The earlier synoptic tradition is clearly more accurate. If further proof is needed, you only have to look back again at the evidence of Luke. In Luke chapter 7, we read that when John the Baptist was put in prison by Herod, he sent two of his disciples to Jesus to ask directly, "Are you the one who is to come, or are we to wait for another?" In other words, the Baptist was still anything but certain that Jesus was indeed the anointed one, the Messiah. This would seem to make little sense if he had personally witnessed the "Spirit descending and resting upon him."

To repeat, then: The source of the accounts of the vision accompanying Jesus' internal transformation – the appearance of the heavens parting, the Spirit's descent, and the voice – must of necessity have been Jesus himself. Unless one subscribes to a fundamentalist-type view of inspiration, that the Spirit simply and miraculously dictated to the writers everything that happened, there is only one way the gospel authors could have come to know about any of it. Jesus told them himself. The same is true of several other important phases in his "call" – most strikingly, of course, his three temptations in the wilderness, when the only record we have says that there was nobody else around to witness and report what went on.

The meaning of the baptismal experience for Jesus

While John's gospel does not mention the heavens opening, or the voice of Divine approval, all three synoptic accounts – Matthew and Luke no doubt following Mark's version – have the following elements: Jesus experiences a mystical vision in which he sees the heavens open (some kind of bursting forth of a great light) and the Spirit descending in a fashion he can only describe as "dove-like." This is accompanied by a voice, which he alone hears; an internal voice, saying, "This is my Son, my beloved. With you I am well pleased." Significantly, Luke alone tells us that it was after he had been thus baptized "and was praying" that this tremendous moment of illumination occurred.

Now when all the people were baptized, and when Jesus also had been baptized and was praying, the heaven was opened, and the Holy Spirit descended upon him in bodily form like a dove. And a voice came from heaven, "You are my Son, the Beloved; with you I am well pleased" (Luke 3:21–2).

What has frequently been passed over lightly or has even been blocked out entirely by many scholars and clergy is the emphasis, especially in Luke, upon the fact that from this critical experience onwards Jesus is "filled with the Spirit of God." The Spirit (God present and active) was always within him from the start. But the baptism and the God-encounter flowing from it reinforced that blessing. Or perhaps better, it kindled it into an open flame. Jesus' new consciousness of a special relationship with the "ground of all being," and of his being "filled" with that presence and energy, came from "above" (it was a transcendent reality) and made itself powerfully felt from within.

As a matter of fact, when it comes to Christology (the attempt to make sense of the divine/human aspects of Jesus Christ), it is this Spirit-based aspect that is the most helpful approach I have yet come upon in many years of study and thought about this vital issue. The perplexing question is, how did the early church eventually come to the complex dogma of the Trinity – the subtleties of which took the best of Greek philosophy to articulate and which is increasingly difficult to communicate to people today? In my view, it is because the plain teaching of the gospels – that Jesus' humanity was fully permeated and moved by his great openness to such a gift, God's spirit or presence – seemed far too simple and obvious. Moreover, this teaching would have failed to meet the various political needs of the Emperor Constantine and his empire at the Council of Nicea, in 325 CE.

One further point. To anticipate a little, this kind of Spirit-Christology not only helps us comprehend the mystery of Jesus, it also is the fundamental solution to the question of how we, too, are heirs of divinity. More on that later.

In spite of speculation, we simply do not know all that led up to this history-changing moment. Luke tells us Jesus was about 30 years old when he began his ministry. Apart from the myths that formed around his nativity, and the questionable historicity of Luke's account of Jesus' discussions with the temple authorities when he was 12 (Luke 2:40–50), the first 30 years of

Jesus' life are correctly called "the lost years." He was obviously raised in a very pious Jewish home in the northern hill town of Nazareth. He was a builder or stone mason like his father. He had plenty of opportunity to see firsthand both the enthusiastic messianism that flourished in the region of the Galilee, and to encounter the secular currents of Greek and Roman culture that flowed along nearby trade routes and that filled the neighboring pagan cities. He had to have been fully aware of the Zealots and of their dreams of armed revolt against the hated Roman overlords; he lived in the Galilee where they were a constant presence.

Incidentally, as is nearly always the case, ancient documents that have occasional gaps or lapses in telling the story of a famous person tend to foster imaginative attempts by others to fill in what is missing. This is certainly the case with the narratives about Jesus. Old and new theories on the "lost years" abound. Some say he went to England with Joseph of Arimathea – hence the Glastonbury Abbey legend, and William Blake's poem "Jerusalem," which includes the words, "And did those feet in ancient time walk upon England's mountains green? And was the holy Lamb of God on England's pleasant pastures seen?" But other accounts have Jesus spending his youth in Egypt acquiring mystical wisdom, or going to monasteries in India and Tibet for the same purpose. The most recent inspired fiction on the subject alleges that Jesus traveled to Japan and formed a community whose descendants still survive. None of these suggestions have much if any serious historical evidence for their claims.

It is impossible to describe the "psychology of Jesus" or to say at what point he became aware of being different from his contemporaries. The evidence for that kind of exploration is simply not there. An unthinking orthodoxy would have us believe he knew of his destiny from the moment of birth – or before. It is assumed his mother would have told him of his unique birth and that at least the two of them were "in" on the secret of who he really was. But this will not stand up to a careful examination of the New Testament documents themselves. I have no intention here of repeating all my reasons for rejecting the Virgin Birth as historical. They are laid out in another book and no critique of those arguments to date has given me reason to doubt their validity. Bishop Spong gives a much more detailed account of the same material in his book *Born of a Woman*.[3]

But it is important to say at least this: I believe that the Virgin Birth is not tenable as an historical fact – its great spiritual value is another matter – not because God couldn't have acted in such a way, but because all the hard evidence we possess shows that God did not. If the literal interpretation of the birth stories, which occur only in Matthew and in Luke (and which differ in some key details), was the correct one and there was indeed a miraculous Virgin Birth, we could agree that Mary the Mother of Jesus would have known it more certainly than anybody else. But the synoptic record makes it abundantly clear that she had no idea of Jesus' special nature and calling until after the Resurrection. The absolute clincher, for me at any rate, comes again from the Bible itself.

In Mark 3:21ff, Jesus' family, including his mother, make two attempts to "restrain" him and to get him to come home and desist from his chosen path of healing and preaching. The Greek says, "For they said, he is beside himself" (in other words, insane). The NRSV makes the "they" to read not as his family, but as people in general. "When his family heard it [about the healings and the great crowds] they went out to restrain him, for people were saying, 'He has gone out of his mind.'" The King James Version tries to avoid the scandal of having his family thinking ill of him by translating verse 21 thus: "And when his friends heard of it, they went out to lay hold on him: for they said, he is beside himself." Later, in verse 31, the family make a second attempt to remonstrate with Jesus. When, however, he is told his mother and brothers are outside and have sent for him, he asks the famous question: "Who is my mother and my brethren?" The point is clear. There is little awareness on Mary's part, at this stage in his ministry, of any special mission or divine nature belonging to her controversial son.

This explains, of course, why the other synoptic gospels completely omit from their narrative the remark about Jesus being thought insane. The entire passage, Mark 3:20–30, is missing from both Matthew and Luke. It's just too embarrassing. Mary and the family in general would never have interfered like this or sought to "restrain" him had she or they prior knowledge of his unique origins and divine status. But certainly Mark would never have included the incident cited above had the incident not been a solid part of his own sources. It remains true that in reading ancient manuscripts one always has more respect for a reading that is difficult and controversial than for one which has obviously been made simpler and smoother. The more difficult reading is always the stronger, preferred one.

One thing we do suspect. Most New Testament scholars today believe that prior to his baptism, Jesus was for a time a follower of John the Baptist. He did not just walk down suddenly from Nazareth one day to the Jordan Valley and ask to be baptized. Once again it helps to look at the Greek text. The words of John the Baptist usually translated as "there is One who is coming after me…" can also mean "there is one of my followers" who is greater than I am. In other words, "after me" does not necessarily have to refer to time. It can and often does refer to place or status. This rendering, I believe, makes better sense. As he followed John and listened to his message of a need for repentance – a turning away from self and sin to God – in view of a coming day of judgment and the arrival of God's Servant who would baptize with the Holy Spirit, Jesus must have felt a growing inner awareness that God was calling him to some as yet ill-defined mission.

I once had the privilege of hiking from Nazareth all the way down the Jordan valley to Jericho, with the Dead Sea always shining to the south, and from there up the winding road through the Judean Wilderness to Jerusalem. I confirmed for myself what I had previously read: that there is an uncanny quality to that vast sweep of often desolate landscape that blows away temporal illusions and confronts you with a sense of the eternal. Heaven and Earth seem stripped clean and bare. Sky, sun, wind, and rock combine to bring you face to face with both yourself and God. It is no accident that three of the world's great religions found their origins in this kind of setting. We need to see that as the extraordinary backdrop for the cataclysmic experience Jesus was about to have.

———

Before continuing, I need to pause for a moment to say something about the use of the term "Son of God," and about Jesus' references to "the Father," in what follows immediately, and in the next chapter as well. I am well aware of the importance of using language that values each person equally before God, regardless of race, creed, or in this particular instance, gender. I am also aware of the importance of using gender-neutral language for God, as one antidote to an oppressive church patriarchy.

My decision to retain the traditional language in what follows is by no means meant to negate or disparage any of this. In fact, the opposite is true. When Jesus is called a "Son of God," or when he refers to himself in this manner, it is not Jesus' male character that is of primary importance, but Jesus' intimate relationship with God. This intimate relationship can be had by all – a crucial point I shall return to later. But to get to that understanding, one needs first to understand what Jesus meant when he identified himself as a "Son of God." In this sense, I approach "Son of God" as a technical term, with a specific meaning I hope to clarify. The same is true of Jesus' references to God as his "Father."

Having said that, let's return again to the important discovery Jesus made at the time of his baptism.

There is no question in my own mind that Jesus had at that moment no sense of a unique sinlessness or of being the Second Person of a Holy Trinity. The texts themselves suggest otherwise. All that sort of doctrine developed, with much argument and plenty of heat, much later. Jesus was, whatever else is claimed for him, a full, human being. I believe he went down into the waters of the Jordan because he felt a need to mark publicly his decision to cease from pleasing self, and to surrender himself wholly to the will of God. As already noted, he was heeding the call of God to repentance and to service, just as the great prophets before him had done, beginning with Moses. Like Isaiah of old, he felt the need of God's cleansing and of the special anointing of God's Spirit. As the Epistle to the Hebrews says,

> *In the days of his flesh, Jesus offered up prayers and supplications, with loud cries and tears, to the one who was able to save him from death, and he was heard because of his reverent submission. Although he was a Son, he learned obedience through what he suffered...*
>
> Hebrews 5:7–8

Then it happened. He waded out into the river to where John was standing and was baptized. He remained praying, talking to God in deep submission to whatever God had in store for him. The vision of light and God's voice suddenly envelops him. He is aware of the Holy Spirit – God's energizing presence, active and overwhelming – coming upon him in a momentously powerful, fresh way. At the same time, the voice, once experienced also by the prophets of old and yet for so long silent in Israel's religious life, speaks within him, though it seems to thunder from the very heavens. It announces that he, Jesus, is God's beloved son, that God has given him total acceptance and approval. He knows for the first time that he is truly at one with Being itself, with the very Author of the cosmos. He enters in the fullest possible degree into the unitive experience which some call "cosmic consciousness." The energy or spirit of the universe, he now fully realizes, is flowing through him. It is a change of consciousness, which profoundly changes everything else.

Today we are aware through the new physics that we are, all of us, expressions of the primal energy and intelligence of the natural world, or of the universe. Authors such as Dr. Deepak Chopra have described this ultimate source of everything, from the galaxies to a field mouse, in bestselling books anyone can understand. Many scientists, especially physicists, now believe there is an infinite, ultimate ground or energy field whose designer and sustainer is God. But ours remains, for the most part, a head knowledge only. For Jesus, at the Jordan, it became a dazzling, experienced reality. In other words, he had made what to him and to the Jewish and Gentile people of his day alike was an amazing discovery – that God, who had spoken of old through the prophets and who was worshipped in the rituals at the temple in Jerusalem, and whom he knew in nature and the scriptures, was actually within him, at one with him. What's more, this God had a unique purpose for him and for his life.

Jesus knew that in the religious language of his people to be recognized as a "Son" or one of the "Sons of God" was to be given the highest possible honor. It meant that one was being called and commissioned for a special service or ministry on God's behalf. It marked a special status and role whose most distinctive characteristic was that of being a person for others. Thus, in the Hebrew Bible, the king was called God's son. Adam was God's son. So too, at times, was the entire nation of Israel in its collective mission. Moreover, in the Book of Job (Job 1:6), it says at the very beginning, "Now there was a day when the sons of God came to present themselves before the Lord, and Satan [the accuser] came also among them." Since that is what the Hebrew text says, I have deliberately used the KJV translation "sons of God" here, instead of the NSRV's much weaker "the heavenly beings." There are several other references in the Old Testament to "God's sons."

SUMMARY

For a more detailed discussion of this highly important term, "Son of God," and of the fact that it need not denote some kind of absolute divinity wholly equal with God and thus seemingly beyond human reach, I refer you to the discussion in *For Christ's Sake,* as well as to Bishop Spong's books, and a list of other authors too numerous to name.

I don't believe that it is possible – in the attempt to determine from a modern perspective what Christianity is all about – to stress unduly the Jordan experience for Jesus. It was the basis for his otherwise scandalous words later in his ministry: "I and my Father are one." Hindus, of course, have no problem with this at all. They believe, as I now do, that it's potentially true of each of us. But the church has failed to emphasize adequately how this radical, transforming insight changed not only Jesus' self-understanding but also his concept of his ministry and of the nature of all human beings everywhere. This crucial failure has occurred even though the Gospel of John, which sets out the highest Christology or comprehension of Jesus' divinity found in the New Testament, is the one that also, in the boldest of language, equates this divine aspect to that possessed by all of us. For those possessed by a need to base everything on the Bible, the following also can't be stressed too much. In John 10:34–36, Jesus quotes the Bible passage in which God says to Israel, "You are all gods and children of the Most High." Jesus goes on to explain that if God could call all those to whom the word of the

Lord had come "sons of God" – and he reminds them of their belief that "the scripture cannot be annulled" – then what is the "big deal" over his own claim, as one sent by God, to be "God's Son"?

To those who arbitrarily dispute the authenticity of any sayings of Jesus they don't care for, and who thus might say that such high-flown words are all made up by some unknown editor or redactor, one has to put the question: How can one account for such striking, extraordinary statements being put into the mouth of Jesus? Would that have been possible if a strand of teaching similar to this were not already well embedded in the oral tradition?

Summing up for now the impact of his baptism vision and calling, we can look at the immediate results. Mark, the earliest gospel, reports that after being assured of his election and calling as God's son, Jesus is "immediately" driven out to the wilderness by the Spirit. Understandably, he needs to have time to reflect upon what has just happened. He needs to assess thoroughly what such a cataclysmic encounter means and how it is to be lived out. It reminds us in a way of Paul who, immediately after his conversion on the road to Damascus, went off to Arabia and stayed for three years before returning and beginning his missionary travels. Since, as already noted, there was nobody with Jesus to make a record of his time of prayer and testing in the wilderness, he is the only possibly source for the description of it. Mark's version is brief and to the point. He was in the wilderness for 40 days – a loaded phrase with all kinds of other scriptural echoes – tempted by Satan; and, "he was with the wild beasts and the angels waited on him." For the other gospel writers, it was a detailed, visionary, mystical experience, which could only be described in Jesus' characteristic style, through vivid symbolism and drama. Luke, the gospel which above all the others stresses the role of the Spirit of God as the agent of Jesus' newly recognized sonship or special relationship with "the Father," says that, after the wilderness retreat, Jesus was "filled with the power of the Spirit" and, returning to Galilee, began his ministry by teaching in the synagogues.

Peter, in an example of the church's earliest preaching, puts it this way in Acts 10:36–38:

> *The word [or Good News] which God sent unto the children of Israel…ye know, which was published throughout all Judea, and began from Galilee after the baptism which John preached; how God anointed Jesus of Nazareth with the Holy Ghost [Spirit] and with power: who went about doing good…for God was with him (KJV).*

His baptism experience was his anointing.

XIII

JESUS' TEACHING

Jesus said:
"The one who is near me is near the fire.
The one who is far from me is far from the Kingdom."
The Gospel of Thomas, Logion 82

God's being is my being
and God's primordial being
is my primordial being.
Wherever I am, there is God.
Meister Eckhart (1260–1329)

If it is correct that the essence of Jesus' breakthrough, discovery, or enlightenment – the reality of his deep unity with the ultimate as a true child of God – was central to his whole self-understanding and mission, it should follow that his teachings directly correspond with such a finding and seek to make it known to all. What is of special significance is the question, "Did Jesus think of himself and his discovery as unique and unrepeatable, or was it something to be claimed and experienced by not just his immediate disciples, but by the whole world of humanity, including you and me?" More specifically, with regard to stress, "Can we hope to discover more fully for ourselves the deep serenity that Jesus felt and knew as a result of such a profoundly liberating change of consciousness?" The answer, I believe, is yes.

THE KINGDOM OF GOD

There can be no doubt whatever that the core and focus of Jesus' preaching and teaching was the kingdom of God, a reality that had come, was presently active in the world, and yet was still to come in the future as well. He didn't come preaching himself but pointing always to the reality of his "Father," by which he meant the transcendent yet immanent Reality, the source and sustainer of everything in the cosmos. According to Mark, as soon as Jesus had been tempted and had heard the news that John the Baptist's ministry was over (Herod had put John in prison, where he remained until he was executed on a whim of the king's wife, Herodias), he came to Galilee proclaiming the Good News of God and saying, "The time is fulfilled, and the kingdom of God has come near; repent and believe in the [this] good news."

This is Jesus' first and main message, no matter what later generations have said.

There is no hint here of future church dogmas. The kingdom of God, or the kingdom of Heaven, a softer term that avoids direct use of the divine name, is the core of it all. It is important to remember that the original language of Jesus was Aramaic, a much more flexible and holistic language than Greek. Thus, in Aramaic, when Jesus refers to the "kingdom," this kingdom is always both within and among us.[1]

John's gospel

John's account, the latest and most theological of the four gospels, is the source most often quoted by proof-texters seeking to uphold the orthodox view of Jesus' unique divinity. Certainly, as already mentioned, it has what must be called a "high" Christology or view of Jesus' person. But it nowhere says Jesus claimed to be God. This brings us back to the matter touched upon briefly a few paragraphs back. It's that crucial passage in the tenth chapter of John's gospel, which has never been given sufficient attention by scholars, clergy, or laity, and especially not by ultra-conservative Christians. Jesus has just said, "I and the Father are one." The authorities then prepare to stone him to death. He tells them he has shown them many good works "from the Father," and asks, "For which of these are you going to stone me?" They reply, "It is not for a good work that we are going to stone you, but for blasphemy, because you, though only a human being, are making yourself God" (John 10:30).

In other words, his claim that he is one with "the Father" is being taken by them – as it is today by many orthodox Christians – to mean that he is claiming to be God. It's at this point that we need to pay very careful attention to the text. Jesus then replies, "Is it not written in your law, 'I said, you are gods'? If those to whom the word of God came were called 'gods' – and the scripture cannot be annulled – can you say that the one whom the Father has sanctified and sent into the world is blaspheming because I said, 'I am God's Son'?" He adds that if they believe he is doing the works of God they should understand from that that he does them because "the Father is in me and I am in the Father."

The passage in the "law" quoted by Jesus is from Psalm 82:6: "I say, 'You are gods, children of the Most High, all of you...'" The King James Version reads: "I have said, Ye are gods; and all of you are children of the Most High." That is to say, those in the past who heard the word of God and who were commissioned by God to act for God were told they were all "gods" and children, or sons, of God. Thus, the charge of blasphemy is of necessity spurious and ridiculous. It cannot be stated too strongly: Jesus here is claiming for himself no more than their own Bible claimed for the prophets before him and indeed for all who were summoned to do God's will.

The truly important point is Jesus' own declaration that to realize and to say that you are one with God or the "Ultimate Source" is by no means a claim to supernatural status or to equality with God. As we shall see, Jesus believed deeply that what he had discovered to be true for himself at his baptism could be and indeed was potentially true for every human being, then and thereafter. God is at one with him; it is God's words he speaks; it is God's mission he has been sent to accomplish. In this, he is perfectly in harmony with the prophetic tradition of the rest of scripture. What is unique and different is the depth of his profound awareness of personal union with this Ultimate Source.

Jesus puts this in various ways. He and "the Father" are one. "The Father" is "in me" and "I am in the Father." Later, in chapter 14, when Philip asks him to "show us the Father," he says that to see him is to see the Father and asks Philip, "Do you not believe that I am in the Father and the Father is in me?" This, again, is emphatically not a claim to absolute divinity. You can know or "see" God at work in Jesus' ministry. Jesus quickly makes this clear by adding that his words are not his own, nor are his works: "The Father who dwells in me does his works." To clinch the argument, he next makes the astounding statement that his followers will not only do the same works as he has done, but also "greater works than these." They, too, will have God, by God's spirit, abiding in them and will be God's commissioned agents or "children." As promised at the beginning of this gospel, all who receive Jesus' message will receive power "to become the sons of God" themselves. The ability to work miracles or "signs," then, is not proof of godhead, as so many have wrongly claimed down the centuries. It is, rather, something potentially open to all who follow Jesus in this same path. Whatever has happened once in human history can happen again. Striking confirmation of this is found in the narrative where Mary Magdalene encounters the risen Christ on the first Easter day (John 20:11–18). She is alone in the garden where Jesus was hastily buried on Good Friday when she sees a man whom she mistakes for the gardener. This person speaks her name. Instantly, she recognizes the voice and calls out, "Rabbouni," or teacher. Jesus immediately tells her not to cling to him, because he has not yet ascended to the Father. Then he says: "Go to my brothers and tell them, 'I ascend to my Father and to your Father, to my God and your God.'" Nothing could be clearer. As reported by this gospel, Jesus makes no distinction between his unity with God and theirs. What is more, their mission is to be exactly the same as his. On his first appearance to the assembled disciples, he tells them explicitly, "As the Father has sent me, so I send you" (John 20:21). Following the prophetic tradition (most notably in the case of Elisha, who asked his mentor Elijah, "Please let me inherit a double share of your spirit"[2]) Jesus then imparts to them the same Spirit in whose power he himself had acted on God's behalf. "He breathed on them and said to them, 'Receive the Holy Spirit...'" We should note that the Hellenistic world was also thoroughly at home with the idea of a person or persons being sent from God for the salvation of others, and being empowered by God for such a mission.[3]

The Prodigal Son

It has already been said that Matthew and Luke both copied large parts of Mark's gospel when it came to writing their own. As noted already, this is why the first three gospels are called synoptic, which means one can look at them side by side and see both the similarities and the differences at the same time. In addition to following Mark, Matthew and Luke use another source, called Q, from the German word, Quelle, meaning source.

Q appears to have been a collection of sayings attributed to Jesus that circulated without a Passion narrative (no account of Jesus' death and resurrection). In addition to Q, Matthew and Luke have some sayings and parables unique to each. In the case of Matthew, this source is called "M"; in the case of Luke, it is called "L." I mention this again because I want next to look at a story or parable that is found only in Luke (and which therefore comes from "L"). I'm referring to the story known as The Parable of the Prodigal Son.

Most of us have read this story or heard it preached about more often than we can remember. Indeed, it has suffered from such overexposure that we may think we know it better than we actually do. Still, most are aware that there are different slants of interpretation taken on this classic story by varying theologians and preachers. For example, we have been told by some that the point of the story is not really about the wastrel, the younger son, but about the elder brother who refused to come to the party, "for he was angry and would not come in."

But here I want to put forward another feature that has been largely or even completely overlooked in any commentary I have ever listened to or encountered in a lifetime of reading. Here is the story from Luke 15:11ff. Having described how the younger son has taken his share of his father's wealth and has wasted it on dissolute living in a "distant country," the account tells how he got a job feeding pigs and "would gladly have filled himself with the pods the pigs were eating." In other words, he had hit rock bottom. "And no one gave him anything." At precisely this point, the narrative reads as follows:

> But when he came to himself he said, "How many of my father's hired hands have bread enough and to spare, but here I am dying of hunger! I will get up and go to my father, and I will say to him, 'Father, I have sinned against

heaven and before you; I am no longer worthy to be called your son; treat me like one of your hired servants...'"

The words that leap out at me whenever I read that passage today are "but when he came to himself." He woke up, came to full consciousness, was enlightened, converted, or whatever term you care to use, the very moment he came to his true or higher self within, and turned away from the shallow, trivial, blinded ego to which he had been committed for so long. Finding the reality of his true, higher self within, he was illumined with the Light he needed to return home and find his earthly father waiting without. The entire parable, as I see it now, is about our roaming in the far country of our appetites and drives – all servants of the ego – until we reach a point where we can of ourselves go no further. Then, by grace and also very commonly by necessity, we are often brought to a grinding halt; we're led in a kaleidoscope of ways to total mindfulness of who and what we truly are. We experience our higher self and realize that we and "the Father" (God, Infinite Mind, Cosmic Intelligence, the Ultimate Source) are one. Like the prodigal, we were lost and have been found. We were "dead" and have been restored to true life. Amazing grace indeed.

The parables of the Hidden Treasure and of the Pearl of Great Price

Matthew's gospel, like Luke's, is filled with parables of Jesus dealing with various aspects of the kingdom of God. Two of these are quite short – each only one verse long compared with Luke's Prodigal Son, which runs for 21 verses. Nevertheless, they speak powerfully of the surpassing value of that reality which Jesus discovered at his baptism but experienced moment by moment of every day.

Here is how Matthew renders them:

*The kingdom of heaven is like treasure hidden in a field, which
someone found and hid; then in his joy he goes and sells all that he
has and buys that field.*

Matthew 13:44

*Again, the kingdom of heaven is like a merchant in search of fine
pearls; on finding one pearl of great value, he went and sold all that
he had and bought it.*

Matthew 13:45

But the treasure and the sensational pearl both stand for the
liberating, life-changing discovery of who one really is – a "child,"
the much-beloved son or daughter of the very font of life.
As the psalmist so eloquently puts it,

*For with you is the well of life;
and in your light shall we see light.*

Psalm 36:9

A great many of the other parables can be seen freshly once one
gains this particular vantage point or perspective. But, of course,
apart from the already quoted passage in John's gospel where
Jesus quotes the scripture, "You are all gods and sons of the most
High," the most direct, clear, and dramatic teaching Jesus ever
uttered on our theme was this familiar logion or saying, "The
kingdom of God is within you."

Let me say this: I have come to believe that this is the key to
both Jesus' teaching and to a Christianity suited to this new
millennium. The liberating, profound wisdom and power held
in these seven simple words surpass anything else in the whole
New Testament. The great tragedy of Christianity lies in the fact
that because of excessive preoccupation with doctrines of sin,
guilt, atonement, redemption, and salvation, this concept of God

already being within us – our original blessing or goodness – has been well-nigh totally neglected.

In Luke's gospel, the Pharisees ask Jesus when the kingdom of God will come. He replies that the kingdom is not something one has to sit and wait for, "For in fact the kingdom of God is within you" (Luke 17:21). (The NRSV translates it as, "among you," and then gives "within you" as an equally sound alternative. The KJV reads, "is within you.") Thomas Berry, the American "ecologian" or "geologian" as he sometimes calls himself, often remarks in his lectures and his books that it is high time the church give up its near-obsessive concern with redemption issues. Instead, it should study and talk about the environment and about what God has revealed in creation or nature, "the first book of revelation." This could radically change how the so-called developed nations deal with the breakdown of the biosphere and, in addition, bring many other incalculable blessings. In a similar fashion, the cultivation of the human soul, the attainment of all that humans are capable of, and a universal joy could rapidly evolve if our theologians and preachers – if the Pope himself – once decided to ease up a little on redemption and to develop a thorough understanding of Jesus' view of himself and of the full nature of humanity.[4]

The kingdom – no airy-fairy ideal

It's important, before moving on, to stress what the kingdom of God or the kingdom of heaven really means. It is, like all language about God, a metaphor and signifies the reign of God as absolute ruler over all. The reign of God, I hasten to point out, is not primarily about power, but about presence. In the oriental world of the ancient Middle East, the monarch's presence extended everywhere and over all of his dominions. There was nowhere his presence could not be seen, through buildings, inscriptions, his effigy on coins, his taxes, his troops, and his edicts.

222 ᴂ FINDING THE STILL POINT

The term "the kingdom of God," then, stands for the living, actively reigning presence of God. (Unlike the ancient kings or emperors, however, God is not a person or a being like other beings, but rather the source and essence of all "beingness" itself.) Jesus' initial proclamation, just after his baptismal experience and the wilderness trials, was that the realm of God was close at hand, there to be realized by all. But the Jewish people's history and their ongoing suffering and oppression said otherwise. Those things told the Jewish people that their hopes were dead, that their God was silent and far off. Jesus bore the good news that these fears were false. His message was that God is in ultimate control, despite appearances to the contrary, and that God was present and active in their hearts. His invitation was to change direction and awaken to this reality within.

Jesus, we notice once again, did not lay heavy theological or dogmatic propositions upon his disciples, or upon the people of his time. All of that took several centuries to develop as later followers wrangled over and finally more or less agreed on what they believed at the Council of Chalcedon, in 451 CE. But Jesus never dealt in philosophical wrangling, in abstractions, in creeds, or in churchy rites. He talked about his relationship with his "Father," and about the relationship of ordinary men and women to this ultimate, loving, cosmic Intelligence. So the kingdom of God, he said, is within you. All that is necessary is to be enlightened with the knowledge of who we really are – children, or "sons" and "daughters," of God. One does indeed need to be born from above.

We have already seen that the same truth is taught in other faiths; The Buddha or the Atman is already within.

XIV

WHAT ABOUT PAUL?

But we have the mind of Christ.

1 Corinthians 2:16

We looked at some of Paul's writings in Chapter 9 when we were considering New Testament resources for use as prayers or mantras aimed at stress reduction in our daily routine. Make no mistake. Whether he be liked or disliked, no objective observer can begin to ignore the profound importance Paul's teaching – or rather, the church's interpretation of his teaching – has had for the development of Christianity. Conservatives, for example, and especially fundamentalists, build almost their entire theology upon texts from his epistles, seldom quoting the gospels except from selected "proof text" passages. All the major traditional Christian doctrines, such as the fall, sin, salvation, justification by faith alone, are attributable ultimately to him. I see him today, however, in what is for me and for many a wholly new way.

True, Paul has been a subject of controversy and the object of anger since the very beginning of the Christian church. In 2

224 ~ FINDING THE STILL POINT

Peter 3:15b–16, the author mentions his "beloved brother Paul." Then, he refers to Paul's letters and notes that, "There are some things in them hard to understand, which the ignorant and unstable twist to their own destruction, as they do the other scriptures." It seems he's referring chiefly to Paul's discussions of Christian freedom from the law and the new life by grace. But plenty of other Pauline passages have had problematic aspects as well, particularly his teachings on women, marriage, celibacy, and sexuality in general.

Apart from that, Paul can sometimes be boastful, ponderous, and insistent on his own way. But nobody can deny that his dynamism, his intellectual power, and his soaring eloquence – never mind his great personal courage and his tough physical stamina – mark him as one of the great heroes of all time. If we had only his magnificent hymn to love in 1 Corinthians 13, it alone would suffice to establish his genius and his profound perception of what true religion, and life itself, are all about – love, or agape as it is called in the original Greek. These words begin what has long been acknowledged as one of the most moving and insightful of all human utterances: "If I speak in the tongues of mortals and of angels, but do not have love, I am a noisy gong or a clanging cymbal…" He was wrong about women; he was wrong about homosexuality being a lifestyle choice. But he was obviously, no matter what other thoughts you, I, or others may have of him, a brilliant, inspired, and deeply spiritual leader.

When it comes to our theme here, the divinity of the human, it might seem at first sight that he has very little to say. He is indeed the shaper bar none of the traditional interpretation of Jesus' meaning in terms of the Second Adam, who rescues humanity from sin and death by faith in his sacrifice, "the blood of the Lamb" and in his Resurrection. For Paul, we are all sinners who, because of disobedience to the Law, deserve eternal separation from God and final extinction (he says absolutely nothing about hell), but whose place in the prisoner's dock has been taken by Jesus Christ. Our sins are cancelled out as Jesus Christ makes Atonement (at-onement) with God, for now and for eternity. As Paul says, "For the wages of sin is death, but the free gift of God is eternal life in Christ Jesus our Lord" (Romans 6:23). Or again, "God proves his love for us in that while we were still sinners Christ died for us. Much more surely then, now that we have been justified by his blood, will we be saved through him from the wrath of God" (Romans 5:8–9).

It is the thesis of retired Episcopalian Bishop John Spong, and of many other key theologians today, that none of this line of thinking makes any sense to modern men and women. I am compelled to agree. It's not that people can't abide talk of sin. It's that the whole paradigm upon which Paul builds his theory of redemption belongs to a much more primitive and bloodthirsty time. As Spong says, it's pre-Darwinian, pre-Freudian, pre-modern mythologizing. Substitutionary "At-onement" through a perfect sacrifice is never going to make it in a modern worldview where science plays so great a part. It may have worked for our parents and earlier ancestors. It may have worked for us for a time. But that time is long ago and we have moved on. It has never worked for me.

Spong puts it bluntly in his 12 theses: "The view of the cross as the sacrifice for the sins of the world is a barbarian idea based on primitive concepts of God and must be dismissed."[1] But the point in any case is that the old, orthodox "take" on Pauline theology is in and of itself myopic and unbalanced if pushed too far, even on its own terms. There is another side to Paul's theology which, for example, flashes tantalizingly before us in his well-known speech to the Athenians on Mars Hill, as described in Acts 17:16–28. We have touched on this briefly before and this is not the place to examine this whole encounter in detail, but the basic outline is this. Paul's fellow travelers, Silas and Timothy, were delayed for a few days at Beroea, where his preaching had caused riots. Paul had been dropped off at Athens to wait for them. While he did so, he spent some time sight-seeing and was appalled at the number of idols he saw. So, as was his habit, he argued with Jews in the synagogue and market-place, and also with Gentile representatives of various philo-sophical schools, Stoics and Epicureans chiefly.

His fame grew and one day the crowd led him to the Ar-eopagus, the famous hill where the law courts stood, to give him a better ambience to make his case. He spoke outdoors in front of the court and used as his contact point an altar he had seen in the city inscribed with the words, "To an unknown god." He began: "What therefore you worship as unknown, this I pro-claim to you." He went on to show how the one God over all does not live in temples or need sacrifices. He is everywhere and all-sufficient, and "gives to all mortals life and breath and all things." This God has made us all from one ancestor or "one blood," he declares. God's aim was that we might live and "search for God…and find him – though indeed he is not far from each one of us. For 'In him we live and move and have our being'; as even some of your own [pagan] poets have said…"

He then makes his point strikingly by an exact quote from pagan sources: "For we too are his offspring" (i.e., we are all children of God – pagans, Jews, Christians, everyone).

Very conservative theologians, mainly fundamentalists, seem to dislike this passage intensely. And because Paul never seems to return to such a natural, universal approach again, they claim he had tried to reach the Athenians on their own terms and found it was a failure to be avoided in future. This is speculation, how-ever. If Luke is reliable at all in Acts, this speech must be taken at face value and assessed as showing that Paul was not nearly as narrow in his outlook as he has been made out to be.

With this background, I want you to consider a most curious phenomenon. Jesus, as we have seen, and as even the most casual reader of the four gospels is forced to conclude, preached and taught incessantly the Good News of the kingdom of God. The phrase, the kingdom of God or the kingdom of heaven, occurs over 40 times in the four gospels. As we have seen, he did it by parables, he did it by aphorisms, and through a plethora of symbols and images. The kingdom was the heart and core, the very essence of what he came to make known. So what does Paul, the lion of the faith, the writer of about one-third of the entire New Testament, the greatest apostle of them all, do with this legacy, this message? Well, according to the account given by Luke in the Book of Acts, at its very conclusion, Paul mentioned it in his teaching to Jewish authorities in Rome when he first arrived there. Luke writes: "After they [the Jewish leaders] had set a day to meet with him, they came to him at his lodgings in great numbers. From morning until evening he explained the matter to them, testifying to the kingdom of God and trying to convince them about Jesus both from the law of Moses and from the prophets" (Acts 28:23). Then, Luke says, Paul spent two years in a hired house, under armed guard, "proclaiming the kingdom of God and teaching about the Lord Jesus Christ with all boldness and without hindrance." And with those words, Acts comes to an end.

However, when one comes to the corpus of Paul's own letters, where we are probably on firmer ground concerning Paul's actual words than in Acts, there is scarcely a mention of the kingdom at all! Compared with the over 40 references to the actual term in the four gospels, and the amount of space there devoted to this subject, Paul's seven or eight very brief, scattered citings of the phrase "the kingdom of God" are remarkably, strangely, few. The entire concept seems peripheral to his main purpose and message.

Here they are:

1. Near the end of his letter to young Christians in Rome, in the final wrap-up, where he discusses the subject of eating food that offends other converts (has not been kosher killed, or in the case of pagans, has first been offered to idols – as all

meat sold in the public markets was), Paul says, "Do not let what you eat cause the ruin of one for whom Christ died…For the kingdom of God is not food and drink but righteousness and peace and joy in the Holy Spirit" (Romans 14:15b, 17).

2. In some fatherly admonitions near the beginning of his first letter to the Corinthian Christians, Paul says he will deal with some members there who have grown arrogant in his absence. He says he will come back soon and will deal not with their "talk" but with their "power." He continues: "For the kingdom of God depends not on talk but on power" (1 Corinthians 4:20).

3. Two chapters later, Paul notes that he has heard of unacceptable behavior in the church at Corinth. He writes: "Do you not know that wrongdoers will not inherit the kingdom of God [at the end]." He then gives a list of the kind of people he has in mind: "fornicators, idolaters, adulterers, male prostitutes," etc. and repeats, "None of these will inherit the kingdom of God" (1 Corinthians 6:9–10).

4. In his highly important chapter, 1 Corinthians 15, on the subject of Jesus' resurrection and the resurrection of the dead in general, Paul finally comes to a description of the "end." This is when "he [Jesus] hands over the kingdom to God the Father." He's talking here, of course, about the kingdom as a semi-political entity, the consummation of God's total reign over all things. As an important aside, it should be pointed out here that it is shortly afterwards, in verse 28 of this chapter, that Paul makes the striking assertion that, "When all things are subjected to him, then the Son himself will also be subjected to the one who put all things in subjection under him, so that God may be all in all." This effectively negates the belief that for Paul Jesus was totally and absolutely equal with God.

5. The last reference in this same letter comes only a few verses later, in verse 50. Paul is speaking of the kind of body that will be able to enter the realm of God's reign beyond this

mortal life. It must be a spiritual body, he insists (so much for the belief that Jesus was raised physically, instead of spiritually): "Flesh and blood cannot inherit the kingdom of God, nor does the perishable inherit the imperishable."

6. In Ephesians 5:5, the apostle is on the same theme we've already touched on in number 3 above. He is making the familiar point that "no fornicator, or impure person, or one who is greedy…has any inheritance in the kingdom of Christ and of God." At the same time, of course, it is plain that the point of writing his letter is to set things right. The "sinners" can repent and be restored.²

7. Finally, Paul speaks briefly of the kingdom (again in the eschatological or "end times" sense) as the full presence and reign of God in the age to come. In 2 Thessalonians 1:5, he tells the Ephesian Christians that their sufferings under persecution are "intended to make you worthy of the kingdom of God, for which you are also suffering." Here again, kingdom is his word for the summing up of all things in the eternal reality of the presence of God.

"IN CHRIST"

Jesus spoke continuously and in detail about the kingdom of God, something he experienced moment by moment in his inner life and in the healing ministry in which he was principally engaged. Paul knows about this teaching and speaks of the kingdom, for example, to the Jewish leaders in Rome, but very rarely in his letters. Even there he does so almost always en passant. The reason for his reticence becomes clear when we dig a little deeper. It all hinges on communication. Since his ministry was not ultimately to Jews but to the Hellenistic world – the world of Ephesus, Corinth, Thessalonica, and first-century Rome – Paul, it appears, discovered early on that the kingdom of God was a fine term to use with his fellow Jews, but it was next to meaningless to a Gentile audience. Like any good communicator, he realized that to make contact with the people he sought to convert he had to speak in their language. He had to use concepts and words easily apprehended by his "target." So instead of the kingdom message, he ran with what is now called Pauline mysticism. His most constant phrase is en Christo, in Christ. Variations of this can be found in his frequent use of companion terms, such as "Christ in you," or having "the mind of Christ." These are clearly synonymous with "walking in the Spirit," or living in the Spirit.[3]

Conservative Christians who complain about changes to the traditional language used to express "the gospel," are often quite startled when shown how Paul, the key evangelizing apostle, made a conscious decision that for the sake of communication the basic teaching of Jesus had to be "translated" or expressed in an entirely new way. And this, even before the gospels were written! It was new wine for new bottles.

At the beginning of the kenosis passage (about the self-emptying or humility of Jesus Christ) in Philippians 2:5, Paul says, "Let the same mind be in you that was in Christ Jesus…"

In 1 Corinthians 2:16, he says also, "But we have the mind of Christ." Elsewhere, he says that if any person be "in Christ," he or she is "a new creation." Further research shows that this kind of union with Christ is found throughout his works as the dominant replacement for kingdom theology. Being one with Christ and having the kingdom of heaven within you are, in truth, the same spiritual reality, in his view. Just as the Spirit of God was in Christ, the source of his divinity, so too this same Spirit is in each of us, the source of our divinity.

In Romans 8:9ff, Paul says, "But you are not in the flesh; you are in the Spirit, since the Spirit of God dwells in you…" A few verses earlier, chapter 8 actually begins with a classic statement of the "in Christ" principle: "There is now therefore no condemnation to them which are in Christ Jesus, who walk not after the flesh, but after the Spirit" (KJV).

In Paul's theology, then, to be "in Christ" or to "have Christ," by the Spirit's presence in us, is identical to the spiritual reality of being in or of the kingdom, to having the kingdom (reigning presence of God) within us. Just as Jesus found, this meant realizing the special relationship each one of us has with God. It meant knowing for oneself that God is, and that we are sharers, as specially created sons and daughters, in his nature. That's why the apostle, in Romans 8, a passage that shows how it is God who, by the Spirit makes this divinity and "childship" actual in us, declares that "all who are led by the Spirit of God are children of God." More, they are thus "heirs of God" as well. This means that we shall all one day be fully gods in God's realm. In fact, Paul here makes his well-known affirmation that we have been given a spirit of adoption whereby our innermost self cries out "Abba! Father!" (Romans 8:14–17a). Abba is the Aramaic, affectionate, and intimate word for one's father. Some translate it, "Daddy."

All of this kind of exposition, a form of mysticism or union-with-God because of Christ's "work" upon the cross, has been thought out carefully by Paul to fit with kingdom teaching from Jesus on the one hand, and with the prominent religious ideas in the Greco-Roman world beyond Judaism on the other. As Karen Armstrong points out in her classic book *A History of God*, Jesus had insisted on the fact that his "powers" and experience of God were not for him alone, but available for all: "Paul developed this insight further by arguing that Jesus had been the first example of a new kind of humanity." He had become the new "Adam" and a fresh start at being a full human being.[4]

XV

CONCLUSIONS

The "poverty" of silence is truly rich in inner and outer peace.
Pure silence holds a wealth of creativity, wisdom,
new energy, and profound compassion.
It above all is the "space" in which God's overwhelming bounty
makes its clearest epiphany to the soul.

Tom Harpur[1]

OUR KEY FINDING

The "still point of the turning world," to quote T. S. Eliot, is another name for the place where God's Spirit and the spirit/mind/body unity of every person come together and are consciously one. This awakening experience which we usually become aware of quite gradually – though sometimes it can explode within with utmost clarity – is where not just Jesus but others of that small group of universal teachers who have graced humankind have discovered their true identity as "children of God." The preceding chapters have argued that this awareness of divinity within and thus of one's full status in the spiritual order, is open and waiting for everyone. This, as Karen Armstrong has learnedly shown in her book *A History of God,* is at heart the underlying cornerstone of all ethical, one-God religions.[2] What's more, to grasp fully and to be permeated by this truth is the fundamental principle in any truly spiritual response to stress, or indeed, to Kabat-Zinn's "full catastrophe" of life itself.

Practicing and developing various meditation skills and other disciplines in awareness of this one, solid worldview or overall outlook on human life and our universe will not, of course, eliminate all stress from anyone's experience. But it absolutely and totally changes the way we answer such basic questions as, "Who am I? Where have I come from? And why am I and all the rest of the world here at all?" It provides a remarkable and health-giving toughness and energy amidst life's vicissitudes, as many scientific experiments and studies have now shown.

One doesn't have to become a formal Christian, Muslim, Jew, or Hindu to awaken to this reality. But we are wired, it seems, for full community and it brings all kinds of tangible benefits to belong somewhere, according to one's proclivities and deep good sense. Being a "light" all alone in one's little corner (I call this "little-corneritis") may be all very well up to a point; but to make the contribution to the good of all for which we are intended – each according to his or her gifts – one needs the encouragement, the flow, the enriching energy available in a wider fellowship of kindred hearts and minds. The relief from stress, the healing that most people are looking for right now – through a thousand different ways – is not an end simply for itself alone. The answer to our former question, "Healing for what?" is not about selfishness or sheer individualism, more of the "me-society" approach. It's about being calmed and strength- ened, no matter what our disabilities may be, so that we may be channels of helping and healing energy to all those around us, especially to those who need it most. It's about service to others and about building a more just, happier global family. It's about being transformed so that the whole of humanity, the race itself, may be transformed. In sum, it cares more about transformation in the present for the sake of the future than about preservation in the present of the past.

But at this point an obvious question demands an answer. What about evil? The tragic and cruel events of September 11, 2001, have indelibly inscribed on every non-terrorist's brain the sheer reality of wickedness or sin, if such a reinforcement of the idea were needed. Are we to say that evil people are "in the image of God" and possess the light of divinity within? The reply to be made, I believe, is a resounding "yes" – with the following explanation.

All faiths agree that one must first awaken to the truth; we must become enlightened as to who we really are before real spiritual life begins. Just as the sun for all its brilliance and power cannot be seen or known on a completely, thickly cloudy day, so too the divine within can be stifled, obscured, or utterly obliterated by denial, a deliberate choice of evil means and ends, or any other of the moral weaknesses that can assail. God forces nobody. The Bible puts it this way: "Listen! I am standing at the door, knocking; if you hear my voice and open the door, I will come in to you and eat with you and you with me" (Revelation 3:20). It always remains the individual's decision. The seed or pilot light of inner "flame" is always there – as with a modern gas fireplace. But it needs a conscious decision to open the blockages and let the fuel through to kindle the real fire.

Here is an outstanding example of what I am talking about. In early December 2001, a Canadian-born Roman Catholic nun who is also a Zen Master, Sister Elaine MacInnes, received the Order of Canada in Ottawa. MacInnes, 77, was awarded this top honor for her years of teaching meditation in prisons in the United Kingdom and the Philippines. She learned Zen meditation – based chiefly on sitting quietly, and regularly, while focusing on the breath – while in Japan as a missionary many years ago. Today she is recognized as one of the world's highest teachers of Zen and finds no conflict whatever between that and her Christian belief. The point is that she has worked with murderers and other serious criminals for years. For example, she once taught meditation to 24 "lifers" at Wormwood Scrubs, one of London's best-known maximum security prisons. She has found that such prisoners, even the toughest and most dangerous, were greatly calmed and made peaceful, and were determined to alter their self-destructive ways after only several weeks of simple meditation practice. MacInnes, with active support from the famous British actor Jeremy Irons, is presently engaged in getting her meditation program into Canadian prisons. About 86 jails in Britain now use it. As she says, "the human heart is universal."[3]

SIGNIFICANCE FOR RELIGION IN GENERAL AND CHRISTIANITY IN PARTICULAR

The results of my research and of my struggle with the themes of this book, not to mention an entire lifetime's involvement in organized religion and 30 years of experience reporting and writing on it, have brought me to the following conclusion: the problem of stress and the attempt to tackle it spiritually, head on, represents a major opportunity for all major faiths. Spirituality, which is not always synonymous with religion but ought to be, can now offer a fresh appeal to rank and file people once its true relevance is made manifest. I believe the time has come when institutions and people of faith should boldly recover their original healing message and make it known as widely as possible. Deep trust in God, in prayer, meditation, silence, and healing rites, has tremendous power both to attract and to hold the interest and keen attention of contemporary men and women. When it comes to running stress clinics with a spiritual approach, the various faiths can work together in their various localities.

Where meditation and healing are concerned they have much more in common than they have things that divide.

There are two other spinoffs:

1. Acknowledgement of and emphasis upon the "divine within" as a universal tenet of faith could lead to a radically new ecumenical spirit spreading around the world. Could not the biblical teaching of the image-of-God-truth or of the various other religious ways of expressing this same reality be seen and understood by all religions and faiths as the basic common denominator binding them all together? Differences in rites, traditions, or dogmas would not matter one iota once this was accepted by all. We're not talking here about melding into one massive world religion, but about deeper harmony and cooperation in serving humanity.

2. Imagine the potential for world peace and justice. Hindus greet one another by a slight bow and a folding together of the hands as if in prayer, to show recognition and respect for the divine within the other person. Suppose that was how every human being saw and understood the true nature of every other person in the world! Fighting and war would become unthinkable. All injustice would stand self-indicted. To harm anyone would be like striking God in the face. All the teachings of the great universal teachers about nonviolence and peace could be fulfilled at last.

Christianity

Karen Armstrong, in the book already cited, says of the apostle Paul, "Paul never called Jesus 'God.' He called him 'the son of God' in its Jewish sense (as an anointed servant of God); he had simply possessed God's 'powers' and 'spirit,' which manifested God's activity on Earth and were not to be identified with the inaccessible divine essence."[4] She adds that the Gentile world of the first century did not "always see such subtle distinctions so

Jesus quickly becomes divine."[5] That is, the Gentile Christians moved easily from his awareness of the divine within to a claim for him of absolute Godhead. In fact, a kind of idolatry has resulted which Jesus himself would have abhorred.[6]

The fresh understanding of Jesus offered here is one which I am convinced is wholly faithful to the New Testament documents, which makes much more sense to our generation than dogmas formulated centuries ago, and which makes Christ truly our brother and not so wholly "other" and remote as church doctrine leads us to believe. Christ's union with God is not a material or metaphysical union, but rather one of deep communion – a *unio mystica* rather than a *unio hypostatica* – a mystical union rather than a union of essence. He manifested forth the divine life as no person had ever done before.

What about the Creeds? The answer I believe is to preserve them as historic symbols and reminders of another day, but to stop trying to force people to repeat them any longer Sunday by Sunday. The earliest "creed" – though it wasn't called one – for the first three centuries of Christianity was quite simply, "Jesus is Lord." As opposed to the then-secular creed of "Caesar is Lord," it called its followers to acknowledge Christ as one's earthly master, guru, and guide. He was the door that led to God. Other cardinal, traditional doctrines need to be changed as well if the church is to survive with integrity into the fullness of this millennium. For example, the dogma that Jesus Christ is the "only" such door.

In most of these issues, I agree with what has already been said by Spong. We must end the current situation in which, as the writer Mihaly Csikszentmihalyi describes it in his book *Flow: The Psychology of Optimal Experience*, "Those who seek consolation in existing churches often pay for their peace of mind with a tacit agreement to ignore a great deal of what is known today about the way the world works."[7] The precise details of all that is entailed in that reality belong to another discussion. I must say here, though, that Bishop Spong's understanding of God in his latest book on the future of a "new" Christianity seems anemic and overly cerebral to me. This is not the "God in our midst" of the Bible or of the Qur'an, or of Hinduism, or, indeed, of my own personal experience.

However, what is of paramount interest in the light of the spiritual approach and responses to stress described in all that has gone before – about the use of the breath, mindfulness, and other forms of meditation, use of the labyrinth and other techniques – is that the churches begin to see the growing anxiety, fear, and confusion of this present hour as a fresh opportunity for reaching out in a relevant and powerful manner to today's generation at the point of need we have identified. It is time to recover and put to use the old, lost jewels in the certainty that the God who dwells within us and who utterly transcends us will lead us on "in newness of life." Churches could begin almost immediately (by baptizing, so to speak, the secular stress clinics) to offer spiritually oriented courses on stress management and begin to put their too-often empty buildings to an immediate, practical use in every community. I prophesy a huge response.

The church need not be moribund. It could change and be born anew – from both within and above.

EPILOGUE

Slow Me Down, Lord

Ease the pounding of my heart by the quieting of my mind.
Steady my hurried pace with a vision of the eternal reach of time.
Give me, amid the confusion of the day,
the calmness of the everlasting hills.
Break the tensions of my nerves and muscles with the soothing
music of the singing streams that live in my memory.
Help me to know the magical, restoring power of sleep.
Teach me the art of taking minute vacations of slowing down to
look at a flower, to chat with a friend,

to pat a dog, to read a few lines from a good book.
Slow me down, Lord, and inspire me to send my roots
deep into the soil of life's enduring values that
I may grow toward the stars of greater destiny.

Anonymous[1]

ENDNOTES

INTRODUCTION
1. Christopher Fry, in *Light of Consciousness* magazine, Spring/Summer, 2001.

CHAPTER 1
1. Allen Klein, *The Courage to Laugh: Humor, Hope, and Healing in the Face of Death and Dying* (Los Angeles: J. P. Tarcher, 1998).
2. *Sports Illustrated*, October 14–20, 2001
3. John Seely Brown and Paul Duguid, *The Social Life of Information* (Boston: Harvard Business School Press, 2000).
4. James Gleick, *Faster: The Acceleration of Just About Everything* (New York: Vintage Books, 2000).
5. Tom Harpur, *Prayer: The Hidden Fire* (Kelowna, BC: Northstone Publishing, 1998).
6. From *Chatelaine* magazine, August, 2000.

CHAPTER 2
1. Jon Kabat-Zinn, *Full Catastrophe Living* ("FCL") and *Wherever You Go, There You Are*, especially the former, pages 150–151, 196–218.

CHAPTER 3
1. Paul Ferrini, *Silence of the Heart* (Massachusetts: Heartways Press, 1996).
2. From the monumental *Zorba the Greek,* by Nikos Kazantzakis. The film was first seen in 1964.

3. Kabat-Zinn, *Full Catastrophe*, p. 1.
4. Ibid., p. 57.
5. Ibid., p. 101.
6. Ibid., pp. 45–46.
7. Ibid., pp. 149–150.
8. Ibid., pp. 166–167.
9. Ibid.

CHAPTER 4

1. From a weekly column on "Transformation," in *The Toronto Star*, August 3, 2001.
2. See Kabat-Zinn, *Full Catastrophe*, pp. 50–52.
3. 1 Corinthians 3:16
4. From a letter to me, July 18, 2001.
5. *Toronto Star*, November 11, 2001.
6. May Sarton, "Invocation to Kali," Section 5, in *May Sarton: Collected Poems (1930–1993)* (New York: Norton, 1993), p. 326. By the way, Mother Teresa's "House of the Dying" in Calcutta is situated within the precincts of a temple of Kali.

CHAPTER 5

1. Thomas Merton, *No Man Is an Island* (Orlando: Harvest Books, 1978).
2. C. S. Lewis, in the *Oxford Book of Prayer* (Oxford: Oxford University Press, 1985), p. 70.
3. C. G. Jung, *Memories, Dreams, Reflections* (New York: Vintage Books, 1989), p. 326.
4. Adam Crabtree, *Trance Zero* (Toronto: Somerville House, 1997).
5. Paul Davies, *The Mind of God* (New York: Touchstone Books, 1992), pp. 222–end.

CHAPTER 6

1. From the "25 Year Retrospective" in *Christian Meditation* newsletter/magazine, January 2000.
2. Marianne Williamson, *A Return to Love* (New York: Harper Perennial, 1992), pp. 190–191.

CHAPTER 7

1. Dag Hammarskjöld, *Markings* (New York: Ballantine, 1993).
2. Lauren Artress, *Walking a Sacred Path* (New York: Riverhead Books, 1996).
3. Robert Ferre, *The Labyrinth Revival* (St. Louis: One Way Press, 1996), p. 5.

4. Ibid., p. 9.

CHAPTER 8

1. George Feuerstein, in *What Is Enlightenment?* magazine, Fall/Winter 2001, p. 44.
2. Karen Armstrong, *A History of God* (New York: Ballantine Books, 1994).
3. For a further discussion of the role of the psalms in a person's prayer life, see *Prayer: The Hidden Fire*, chapter 6, "Prayers with 'Suction.'"
4. William Bliss Carman, as quoted in *Bartlett's Familiar Quotations*.

CHAPTER 9

1. *The Secret Sayings of the Living Jesus* (Waco, TX: Word Books, 1968).
2. Chapters 5–7, especially chapter 5:43–8.
3. See Matthew 5:43–48.
4. Without getting bogged down in too much detail, here are some of the more obvious differences between John and the three other gospels. There are few parables. The account of the institution of Holy Communion or the Mass is missing and replaced by the washing of the disciples' feet. Like Mark, there is no nativity story and no virgin birth. The cleansing of the Temple comes right at the beginning of Jesus' ministry and not at the end where the others all have it. The amazing story of Lazarus is unique to John. The style is different, etc.
5. If you've never read Henry Drummond's book *The Greatest Thing in the World* (Nashville: Nelson Reference, 2000), I strongly recommend it.
6. For further elaboration of this theme see Ephesians 4:25 – 5:20 and, indeed, the entire corpus of Pauline letters.

CHAPTER 10

1. Tulku Thondup, *The Healing Power of Mind: Simple Meditation for Exercises for Health, Well-Being, and Enlightenment* (Shambhala, Boston, 1996), p. 19.
2. *The Oxford Book of Prayer*, #922, p.303. Subsequent references to this volume will be identified in the text as follows: OBP, page number.
3. *Healing Through Prayer*, p. 141.
4. Ibid.
5. Ibid., p. 142.
6. From Pema Chodron, an American Buddhist NUM and resident teacher at Gampo Abbey, a monastic center for both men and women in Cape Breton, Nova Scotia. Instructions given to a 12th-century Tibetan Buddhist yogini, Machik Labdron, by her teacher.

7. *How to Know God, The Yoga Aphorisms of Patanjali,* trans. William Q. Judge (Theosophy Co., 1930), p. 56. Subsequent references to this volume will be identified in the text as follows: Patanjali, page or instruction number.
8. *The Upanishads – Breath of the Eternal,* trans. Swami Prabhavananda and Christopher Isherwood (Hollywood: Vedanta Press, 1981), p. 14. Subsequent references to this volume will be identified in the text as follows: Upanishads, page number.
9. *The Toronto Star,* December 3, 2001
10. *The Oxford Book of Prayer,* p. 331.
11. Ibid., Sura 1.1, The Fatihah or Opener. Subsequent references to this volume will be identified in the text as follows: OBP, Sura number.
12. *The Holy Qu'ran,* trans. Maulawi Sher'Ali (Calcutta: The Statesman Commercial Press, 1971), Sura 2:187. Subsequent references to this volume will be identified in the text as follows: HQ, Sura number.

CHAPTER 11

1. Martin Buber, *The Way of Man* (Lyle Stuart, 1995).
2. Alfred Lord Tennyson, "The Two Voices," stanza 69.
3. Tom Harpur, *For Christ's Sake* (Toronto: Oxford University Press, 1986), p. 123.

CHAPTER 12

1. Baba Hari Dass, *Fire Without Fuel* (Santa Cruz: Sri Rama Publishing, 1986).
2. See Acts 18:24–28 for its references to Apollos.
3. John Spong, *Born of a Woman: A Bishop Rethinks the Birth of Jesus* (San Francisco: HarperSanFrancisco, 1994). See also *For Christ's Sake* pp. 26–31, 68.

CHAPTER 13

1. See Neil Douglas-Klotz in his wonderful little book, *Prayers of the Cosmos – Meditations on the Aramaic Words of Jesus* (San Francisco: HarperSanFrancisco, 1994), pp. 2–3.
2. Kings 2:9
3. See C. K. Barrett, *The Gospel According to St. John* (London: SPCK, 1962), p. 474, notes on John 20:21.
4. Refer to Matthew Fox in *Original Blessing* (New York: Putnam Publishing Group, 2000).

CHAPTER 14

1. John Spong, *Why Christianity Must Change or Die* (San Francisco: HarperSanFrancisco, 1999), Thesis # 5.
2. See Galatians 5:21 and the repetition there of blatant sinners being unfit to "inherit the Kingdom of God."
3. Galatians 5:25.
4. See Armstrong, *A History of God*, p. 88 and throughout, for the theme of the ultimate union of the human and the divine in all religions.

CHAPTER 15

1. Tom Harpur, personal diary, April 14, 2001.
2. Armstrong, *A History of God*, throughout, but see especially p. 178.
3. *Toronto Star*, November 28, 2001, p. B1.
4. Armstrong, *A History of God*, page 83.
5. Ibid., pp. 83–86.
6. Ibid., p. 15. Paul and Silas were mistaken as the gods Zeus and Hermes, in Acts 14:11–18.
7. Mihaly Csikszentmihalyi, *Flow: The Psychology of Optimal Experience* (New York: HarperCollins, 1991), p. 14.

EPILOGUE

1. Found on an old poster in Aurora United Church, Aurora, Ontario, September 2001.

BIBLIOGRAPHY
AND SUGGESTED READING

Appleton, George, General Editor. *The Oxford Book of Prayer*. Oxford: Oxford University Press, 1985.

Armstrong, Karen. *A History of God*. New York: Random House, 1997.

Artress, Canon Lauren. *Walking a Sacred Path – Rediscovering the Labyrinth as a Spiritual Tool*. San Francisco: Berkley Publishing Group, 1996.

Benson, Herbert, M.D. *Timeless Healing: The Power and Biology of Belief.* New York: Simon and Schuster, 1996.

Cassell, E. J. *The Nature of Suffering and the Goals of Medicine*. Oxford: Oxford University Press, 1991.

Chodron, Pema. *Start Where You Are: A Guide to Compassionate Living*. Boston and London: Shambhala, 2001.

—— *The Wisdom of No Escape – and the Path of Loving-Kindness*. Boston and London: Shambhala, 1991.

—— *When Things Fall Apart*. Boston and London: Shambhala, 2000.

Chopra, Deepak. *How to Know God: The Soul's Journey into the Mystery of Mysteries*. New York: Harmony Books, 2000.

Crabtree, Adam. *Trance Zero: Breaking the Spell of Conformity.* Toronto: Somerville House, 1997.

Csikszentmihalyi, Mihaly. *Flow: The Psychology of Optimal Experience.* New York: Harper Perennial, 1990.

Das, Lama Surya. *Awakening the Buddha Within: Tibetan Wisdom for the Western World.* New Hampshire: Broadway Books, 1998.

—— *Awakening the Buddhist Heart: Integrating Love, Meaning and Connection into Every Part of Your Life.* New Hampshire: Broadway Books, 2000.

——*Awakening to the Sacred: Creating a Spiritual Life from Scratch.* New Hampshire: Broadway Books, 1999.

Dossey, Larry. *Healing Through Prayer.* Toronto: Anglican Book Centre, 1999.

Ferre, Robert. *The Labyrinth Revival.* St. Louis: One Way Press, 1996.

Ferrini, Paul. *The Silence of the Heart: Reflections of the Christ Mind.* Two Parts. Massachusetts: Heartways Press, 1996.

Foster, Richard. *Celebration of Discipline: The Path to Spiritual Growth.* San Francisco: HarperSanFrancisco, 1988.

Frankl, Viktor. *Man's Search for Meaning: An Introduction to Logotherapy.* London: Hodder & Stoughton, 1987.

Harpur, Tom. *Prayer: The Hidden Fire.* Kelowna, B.C.: Northstone Publishing, 1998.

—— *For Christ's Sake,* reprint edition. Toronto: McClelland & Stewart, 1993.

Holloway, Richard. *Dancing on the Edge: Faith in a Post-Christian Age.* London: Fount Paperbacks, 1997.

Holy Bible, New Revised Standard Version (NSRV). Grand Rapids, Michigan: Zondervan Publishing House, 1989.

Kabat-Zinn, Jon. *Full Catastrophe Living.* New York: Bantam Doubleday Dell Publishing Group, Inc., 1990.

—— *Wherever You Go, There You Are: Mindfulness Meditation in Everyday Life.* New York: Hyperion, 1994.

Lonergan, Sig. *Labyrinths, Ancient Myths & Modern Uses.* Glastonbury, U.K.: Gothic Image Publications, 1996.

Lynch, James J. *A Cry Unheard: New Insights into the Medical Consequences of Loneliness.* Baltimore: Bancroft Press, 2000.

Moss, Jeffrey. *Oneness: Great Principles Shared by all Religions.* New York: Ballantine Books, 1989.

Myss, Dr. Caroline. *Anatomy of the Spirit: The Seven Stages of Power and Healing.* New York: Random House, 1997.

Norden, Dr. Michael. *Beyond Prozac.* New York: HarperCollins, 1996.

Nouwen, Henri J. *The Way of the Heart.* New York: Ballantine Books, 1991.

Prabhavananda, Swami, and Isherwood, Christopher. *How to Know God: The Yoga Aphorisms of Patanjali.* Hollywood: Vedanta Press, 1981.

—— *Bhagavad-Gita: The Song of God.* New York: Mentor Books, 1944.

—— *The Upanishads: Breath of the Eternal.* New York: Mentor Books, 1948.

Spong, John. *A New Christianity for a New World.* New York: HarperCollins, 2001.

—— *Here I Stand: My Struggle for a Christianity of Integrity, Love and Equality.* San Francisco: HarperSanFrancisco, 2000.

—— *Why Christianity Must Change or Die: A Bishop Speaks to Believers in Exile.* San Francisco: HarperSanFrancisco, 1999.

Thondup, Tulku. *The Healing Power of Mind.* Boston and London: Shambhala, 1996.

Vardi, Lucinda. *God in All Worlds.* Toronto: Alfred A. Knopf, 1995.

Williamson, Marianne. *A Return to Love.* New York: Harper Perennial, 1992.

INDEX

H

healing **14, 42, 63, 117, 118, 125, 127, 132, 152, 161, 168, 236**
 for what? **234**
 holistic **13**
 labyrinth **99**
 path of **204**
Hebrew Bible **106**
hell **134, 224**
 literal **184**
Heraclitus **17**
Hinduism **45, 150, 167, 168, 171, 234 , 237, 239**
holistic **28, 29, 31, 41**
Holy Spirit **205, 207, 210, 217**

I

Information Age **11, 22**
 infoglut **11**
Islam **9, 58, 172, 173**

J

Jesus **32, 40, 63, 76, 84, 109, 131-148, 154, 185-188, 194-195, 204-210, 224, 230-233, 237-238**
 healing ministry **229**
 Jewish **203**
 teaching of **213, 230, 231**
Jew **61, 147, 226, 234**
Jewish **84, 152, 208, 237**
 spirituality **107**
John, the apostle **146**
John, gospel of **146-147, 151, 167, 184, 185, 198-199, 209, 215**
John the Baptist **115, 198, 199, 200, 205, 214**
Joshua **111, 113**

Judaism **9, 58, 231**
Julian of Norwich **64**
Jung, Dr. C. G. **29, 65, 136**

K

Kabat-Zinn, Jon **30-31, 35-36, 41-43, 46, 78, 101, 106, 234**
King James Version **59, 147, 204 215**
kingdom of God **62, 132, 137, 145-148, 188, 194, 214, 219-222, 226-229**
Küng, Hans **60**

L

labyrinth **85, 87, 239**
 Cnossos **87**
 Greek mythology **88**
 healing **96, 99**
 mantra **99**
 meditation **90**
 Orlando, Florida **93**
 path of prayer **93, 95**
 path of silence **95**
 prayer **99**
 silence **91**
 spiritual tool **89**
 St. Louis Labyrinth Project **100**
 stress reduction **92**
 transformation tool **100**
 Woodlawn Memorial Park **93**
Lewis, C. S. **61, 62**
liberals **189**
literal **62, 128**
 hell **184**
 Virgin Birth **173, 193**
literalist **58**